FLY. NO FEAR!

A Handbook For Apprehensive Flyers

written by

Captain Adrian Akers-Douglas

and Dr George Georgiou PhD

cartoons by Matt Wilde

SUMMERSDALE

First published 1996.

Summersdale Publishers
46 West Street
Chichester
West Sussex
PO19 1RP
England

A CIP catalogue record for this book is available from the British
Library.

ISBN 1 84024 006 7

Printed in Great Britain by Antony Rowe Ltd, Chippenham, Wiltshire

The writers hope that this book will be of some help to the very many
people for whom flying is a fearful ordeal. We are grateful to the
numerous passengers who have helped with advice, suggestions, or by
divulging their special concerns. If anyone who reads this has any
comments (favourable or unfavourable!), we should be very pleased
to hear from them. Please write to the address below: Captain Adrian
Akers-Douglas, P. O. Box 257, Limassol, Cyprus.

Contents

Introduction

The writers hope that this book will help the many people who are apprehensive about flying. It has been estimated that about one person in five falls into this category: far more than care to admit it openly!

Sometimes unnecessary anxiety is caused by events about which professional aircrew have become blasé. Pilots and Cabin Crew may take for granted aspects of flights which are mystifying and even alarming to less frequent flyers. Part I of this book takes readers through a typical flight, explaining in non-technical terms just what is happening at any point in the journey. This is followed by Part II, a 'Chamber of Horrors' section, which deals frankly with some of the aspects of flying which may be a cause of worry.

Part III offers a professional explanation, in easily understandable terms, of the phenomena which cause anxiety and offers an unusual perspective on dealing with it. This section gives apprehensive passengers a step-by-step, easily-followed, and practical system of alleviating their fears.

Two appendices offer further advice on dealing with fear of flying, and an index at the back will help you to look up quickly those aspects which especially interest you.

If this little publication helps readers to come to terms with an extremely safe form of travel, it will have fulfilled its function. Part of the royalties from sales are being donated by the authors to charitable causes, including the Cyprus Conservation Foundation, a charity which is promoting conservation and environmental awareness on the island.

PART I

The Flight Now Departing . . .

In the Beginning:

Centre of Attention

As you leave home to check in for your flight, the professionals who will be responsible for your comfort and safety will probably already be at work. You may have seen how an aircraft becomes the centre of a hive of activity when it lands. Baggage and catering is unloaded and loaded, fuel and drinking water are pumped on, the cabin is cleaned and readied for the next flight, and a series of checks performed.

Unlike a car, aircraft are usually serviced on a continuing basis. Whenever they land, certain checks and examinations will be undertaken. Then at prearranged intervals the aircraft is taken out of service for a few hours, days, or even weeks while ever more elaborate maintenance is carried out.

Crew Briefing

Whilst the engineers, caterers, cleaners, baggage handlers, and refuellers are attending to the aircraft, the flight deck and Cabin Crews will be reporting for their briefings. These usually start about an hour before the flight is due to depart.

Planning

The Flight Deck crew assemble in an office where they are supplied with all the details concerning the flight: the weather en-route and at the destination; the number of passengers and the weight of freight being carried; a computer-generated plan of the route, predicting the flight time and fuel needed; details of any technical problems on the aircraft; and any information which might affect the route which the crew plan to take.

The Captain then decides on the amount of fuel to be loaded, which will be enough to fly to the destination, then to another airfield should the destination, for any reason, be closed when the flight arrives, and an extra amount on top of that. (See also 'FUEL' on page 34)

Simultaneously, a 'Flight Plan', giving details of the time and height at which the aircraft will pass over various points along the route, together with its estimated time of arrival at the destination, is sent by the airline's Operations Department to all the Air Traffic Control Centres responsible for regulating the flow of traffic along the route which the flight will take. These Centres then start to integrate 'our' flight with all the others which will pass along the same route at the same time.

Eventually, the Operations Department will be given a time at which the flight must depart in order to fit in with the other traffic. Usually, this is very close to the scheduled departure time.

Cabin Crew

Whilst the Flight Deck crew complete their briefing, the Cabin Crew leader will be ensuring that his or her colleagues are fully aware of what they have to do in any emergency, that they know where all the related equipment is to be found on the aircraft, and how to operate it. Only then will they turn to how they intend to conduct the passenger service, the needs of any special cases (handicapped people, unaccompanied children, etc) who will be on board, and any specific details relating to the flight.

The cabin crew will discuss the needs of unaccompanied children

At least half an hour before the flight is due to depart, the crew will go out to the aircraft. The Cabin Crew check the emergency equipment, such as fire extinguishers, medical kits, and the portable oxygen bottles which are kept in the cabin (for use if a passenger is taken ill), and then they ensure that all the catering and bars are in order. They will also complete the 'dressing' of the cabin: arranging the seat belts tidily, placing antimacassars on the head-rests, etc.

Checking the Aircraft

Meanwhile, the pilots will be running through an exhaustive series of checks on the various aircraft systems, loading the day's flight information into the computers, tuning in the radio navigation beacons which they will need for the departure, and checking the day's route on their maps. One of the pilots will also walk around the outside of the aircraft, double checking an inspection which has already been carried out by the Ground Engineers.

Eventually the crew will report that they are satisfied with the condition of the aircraft, and the passengers will be called. By the time the 'customers' arrive, much of the activity around the aircraft will have subsided, although there will probably still be last minute baggage and freight to load, and if you look into the Flight Deck as you board, you may see the crew still busy with their checks.

When everyone is on board, the Cabin Crew count heads.

It is important that exactly the number of passengers expected are actually on board. Too many: probably someone has got on the wrong flight. Two few, and a 'baggage identification' procedure has to be implemented to ensure that no-one has checked in any luggage and then 'disappeared'. In these days of random terrorism, such risks are unacceptable.

Doors Closed

If the passenger count is correct, the Captain signs the documents which confirm the satisfactory state of the aircraft and its systems, the weight of the aeroplane, and where its centre of gravity lies. The last of the ground personnel leave, and the doors are closed.

You may then hear the Cabin Crew leader telling his staff to 'Arm the slides' or 'Arm the doors'. Each of the doors and the over-wing exits are equipped with slides to help people escape from the cabin in the event of an emergency landing. These slides are inflated by compressed air (sometimes they can also be used as life-rafts if the aircraft has to land on water). When the slides are 'armed', they will automatically inflate when the doors are opened.

There is little quite so embarrassing as forgetting to 'disarm' the slides after landing, arriving at the terminal, opening the door, and watching aghast as a writhing rubber slide unwinds in front of the bemused passengers and ground staff! Thus it is essential that the Cabin Crew check that the slides are 'disarmed' after the aircraft has landed safely at its destination.

A writhing rubber slide unwinds

Starting Up:

'Clear to Start'

The pilots will then call the Control Tower for permission to start engines. Providing all the Air Traffic Control Regions through which the aircraft will pass, and the destination airport, can accept the flight without delays, permission to start will be given.

If, on the other hand, the airspace along the route is congested, we may suffer one of those tedious delays awaiting a place in the queue. If this happens, and the delay is going to be lengthy, the Captain will contact the airline's Operations Office to try to work out an alternative routing which may be less busy. This sometimes works, but at other times, especially at peak holiday periods, there is just such a volume of traffic that all routes are jammed. Then patience and good humour are the qualities most in demand from passengers and crew.

Despite the more lurid accounts in the popular press, serious delays (more than about 15 minutes) are relatively infrequent. With permission to start granted, the flight really comes to life, accompanied by what may seem to some people like rather alarming whines, clunks, whirs, and various other sounds.

'Start Engines'

Perhaps the first indication which a passenger notices that the engines are being started is when the flow of conditioned air to the cabin is cut off.

This is because the engines on most aircraft are started using compressed air from the same source that supplies the air conditioning - a small jet engine (called an Auxiliary Power Unit, or APU) usually located in the tail of the airliner. This little motor, which allows the aircraft to be independent of ground services, supplies electricity, hydraulic power (to operate the brakes and the doors of the cargo holds), and air conditioning. During start up, the APU cannot provide enough air for both air conditioning and the engine starter system, so the cabin conditioning is shut off for the short time it takes to get the engines going.

The aircraft often trembles slightly as the engines gather speed and the cabin lights may flicker briefly as the engine-driven generators take over the supply of electricity from the APU. Once the engines have started, you may hear a series of strange rumblings, whirs, and clunks apparently coming from underneath the floor of the cabin. These are caused by the pilots moving the 'slats' and 'flaps' into the position required for take-off.

'High Lift Devices'

'Slats' and 'flaps' are the bits which droop down from the front and back of the wing on take-off and landing. Flaps hang down at the back of the wing, and slats at the front (not all aircraft have slats). They are known as 'high lift devices'. What are they for?

Aircraft wings are a compromise which have to meet two different requirements. During the cruise at high altitude we want the aeroplane to fly fast. This requires a certain shape of wing. But when we are taking-off and landing, we want to fly slowly, so that we do not use up too much runway. This requires a completely different shape of wing. Since no-one has yet invented the fully flexible rubber wing, the designers arrange a compromise by fitting slats and flaps to the wing, which effectively alter its shape to fit the phase of flight.

These slats and flaps are electrically or hydraulically operated, which accounts for those whirs and clunks as they move into position. It also accounts for similar whirs and clunks as the pilots retract the slats and flaps after take-off.

The flight deck crew complete a series of checks after the engines are started, and then get permission from the control tower to taxi out to the runway.

Wheels Rolling

If you are sitting near a window, you may see the Ground Engineer, who has supervised the start-up, waving the crew off and perhaps holding up what appears to be a broad red ribbon. This is attached to a finger-sized pin, which is inserted into the nose-wheel assembly while the aircraft is pushed back from its parking stand. This pin disables the nose-wheel steering system, so that the tractor which pushes the aircraft back does not damage the aeroplane's steering mechanism. The crew want to know for sure that the Ground Engineer has pulled this pin out and thus restored their ability to steer the aircraft on the ground, which is why he waves the red ribbon at them.

The ground engineer waves the aircraft off

As the aircraft taxies out, you may be able to see some of the results of the checks the crew are performing. You will see various surfaces rising and falling on the wing as the pilots check the controls. As they proceed towards the runway, the crew will also be receiving from the Control Tower their instructions for the departure and the route to be followed for the flight. Whilst all this is going on, the Cabin Crew will be showing the passengers what to do if an emergency should occur during the flight: the aviation equivalent of the traditional nautical 'boat drill'.

Safety Drills

It really is worth paying attention to these demonstrations. In the extremely unlikely event of something happening during the flight, there may not be time to repeat all this briefing. How many of those people with their heads buried in newspapers during the pre-takeoff demonstration will know where to find the emergency exits or how to put on their oxygen masks? Apart from anything else, it is pretty soul-destroying for the Cabin Crew to be performing in front of a completely disinterested audience!

Eventually, everything is ready in the cockpit, the cabin, and with the Air Traffic Control authorities. The flight is cleared for take-off. For the pilots, this and the landing are the two best moments in the whole flight. Those who are apprehensive of flying may not share our enthusiasm for this experience, which is always exhilarating, no matter how often we have done it.

Take-off

Take-off and landing are the two most critical phases of the flight, simply because these are the times when the aircraft is closest to the ground. Aeroplanes and terra firma do not mix well: it is extremely rare for disaster to befall an aircraft high in the sky - it is when it meets the ground in unscheduled fashion that catastrophe ensues. On take-off, the aircraft must accelerate from rest to a speed at which it will fly - typically about 160 mph in a jet - in a bit over a mile. The pilots therefore set the engines to their take-off power quite quickly, resulting in a surge of thrust pushing you back against your seat.

Engine Power

On the most modern aircraft, the engine power is set automatically, by simply pressing a button. A computer then selects exactly the power needed, which is usually less than the engines' maximum capability. In just the same way that it is not good practice to put the accelerator in a car 'flat to the floor', so the pilots can reduce the wear and tear on their engines by only using as much power as is actually required taking into account the prevailing conditions (the weight of the aircraft and the wind and temperature at the airfield).

The maximum power available from modern jet engines is awesome: it is hard to give valid comparisons, but a large engine like a Rolls Royce RB211 produces a power output equivalent to that of about 46 family cars.

In the passenger cabin, the start of the take-off is marked by a rising whine from the engines, a distinct push in the back due to the formidable rate of acceleration, and sometimes a slight popping of the ears. This latter sensation is caused by the pressurisation system which, in some aeroplanes, ensures that the air pressure on take-off inside the cabin is higher than the atmospheric pressure outside. This 'pre-pressurisation' of the cabin means that, should the aircraft have an accident on take-off, the higher pressure inside the cabin will ensure that no fuel vapour, fumes, or smoke can get into the passenger compartment.

What if . . . ?

As the aircraft races down the runway, the crew will be monitoring the instruments for the slightest sign of a malfunction, and will be checking that the aircraft is accelerating normally.

People often ask: 'What happens if an engine fails during the take-off?' The answer is 'Nothing terribly dramatic'. The fact is that the pilots are expecting an engine to fail at the most critical point of the take-off! If this sounds like just the sort of titbit to put you off flying forever, let's explain a bit of the philosophy which lies behind all aircraft design and flying training.

If something goes wrong when driving a car, you can just pull in to the side, stop, and sort the problem out. This option is, of course, not available when cruising 7 miles high, so very elaborate (and very expensive) efforts are made to ensure that nothing goes wrong with the aircraft, or, if it does, that the crew are capable of dealing with any situation that confronts them.

Safety First

Thus, on an aeroplane, any system of importance is duplicated, triplicated, or even quadruplicated. If one should fail, there is another to take over. Typically, a twin-engined aircraft will have three generators to provide the necessary electricity, any one of which would be sufficient for the aeroplane's needs. If the whole lot quit, there are powerful batteries in reserve. The controls are worked by hydraulic power from three separate systems, and again any one of these would be enough. If they all give up, there is a fourth, emergency system which would ensure that the aircraft could be flown to a safe landing. And so on. Very much a 'belt and braces' concept.

The Right Stuff?

But ultimately the safety of each flight lies in the hands of the crew, no matter how sophisticated the aeroplane may be. So airlines spend very large sums of money training their crews to extremely high standards. Indeed, aircrew are probably one of the few professions in the world in which the individual's proficiency is constantly being reviewed.

A pilot typically undergoes at least seven medical or flight checks each year, during which he or she will be required to demonstrate a high degree of skill, knowledge, fitness, and resourcefulness. And to ensure that there are no 'cosy arrangements' whereby colleagues within an airline set lenient standards for each other, the airlines themselves are independently supervised by government civil aviation inspectors, who periodically sit in on these examinations and ensure that all is above board and that a high standard is maintained.

The reason that the airlines spend so much money training their crews and keeping up their proficiency is that the crews are expected to cope with anything which happens, no matter how unlikely the probability of it occurring. Thus, we always assume the worst - for example that an engine will fail on take-off, and that it will choose the worst possible moment to do so.

The crew therefore ensure before departure that the weight of the aircraft is limited to not more than that at which the take-off could be continued safely (after a certain speed is reached) even if the wretched engine does buck tradition and fail. Actually, engines very rarely do fail, especially at the most critical point in the take-off. (Except in the training simulator, when Cruel and Sadistic Instructors arrange that everything goes wrong almost all the time. You will learn later in this publication about the ghastly sufferings inflicted on your lovable Flight Deck crew by these CSI's. See pages 43 & 44).

All Systems 'Go'

Anyway, back to the take-off. As the aircraft gathers speed, the crew will be very closely monitoring that everything is normal.

The pilot flying the aircraft will be handling the controls (there is no such thing yet as an 'automatic' take-off), whilst the other pilot scans the instruments and calls out certain speeds as they are reached.

The most important of these is called 'V1', or Decision Speed. Below this speed, if anything goes wrong we abandon the take-off and stop. Above this speed, we are going too fast to bring the aircraft to a halt on the remaining length of runway, so it is safer to continue with the take-off, resolve the problem once we are airborne, and then decide whether to continue with the flight or return to land. As we have mentioned before, even if an engine fails at 'V1', the take-off can be continued perfectly safely, a manoeuvre we regularly practice in the flight simulator.

The next speed the crew are looking for is the 'Rotation Speed'. This will be a bit higher than 'V1', and is the speed at which the aircraft can be lifted off the runway. It is called 'Rotation Speed' because this is literally what the pilot handling the controls does: he eases back on the control column, the nose of the aircraft rises, and within moments we are airborne and climbing away from the runway.

Up, Up, and Away

In modern aircraft, the initial rate of climb, and angle of the aircraft, can appear very steep. In fact the actual angle will be a bit less than 20 degrees from the horizontal, but it can feel like much more as you are tilted back in your seat.

As soon as the pilots are certain that the aircraft is clear of the ground and is climbing normally, they raise the wheels. This often leads to a series of whines and thumps as the hydraulic system opens and closes the undercarriage doors, and heaves the heavy wheel assemblies into their cavities.

A minute or so later, more whirs and clunks may announce that the time has come to retract the slats and flaps. If you are sitting near the wing, you can see these surfaces sliding into position.

The aircraft will now be accelerating and climbing fast, but in a busy control zone, such as those around major airports, the crew are often instructed by Air Traffic Control to interrupt the climb to allow other departing or arriving aircraft to pass above them. This can sometimes cause alarming changes in engine noise or aircraft attitude as the pilots level off, reduce engine power (so as not to go too fast), and then increase the power and pull up into a climb again when they are cleared to do so.

'Aluminium Overcast'

If you are sitting beside a window, you may also see other aircraft passing apparently very close to you. In fact, the vertical separation between aeroplanes at these lower heights is always at least a thousand feet. However, a Jumbo jet passing a thousand feet above you looks very impressive: the sight is known in aviation circles as 'aluminium overcast'.

The aircraft will soon be clear of the busy area around the airport, and then the climb is usually a smooth and steady ascent to a height of between 31,000 and 39,000 feet, depending on how heavy the aircraft is and which way it is travelling. Aeroplanes are separated by at least two thousand feet vertically at cruising heights. It normally takes about 20 minutes to climb to the initial cruising height, and when the aircraft levels off, the change of attitude is often so slight as to be almost imperceptible, although you may hear the engine note change as power is reduced to that needed for level flight.

Later on during the trip, as fuel is burned off and the aircraft becomes lighter, the crew may climb again, because generally speaking jet aircraft perform best when flying as high as their weight allows.

The maximum height at which a jet airliner can fly varies from type to type, but is usually around 41,000 to 43,000 feet. Concorde trundles along at about 60,000 feet, an appropriately rarefied altitude from which to look down on the peasants below.

The Cruise

The cruising part of the flight, which may last from just a few minutes to interminable hours on a long journey, is generally pretty boring for the passengers. That is why the airlines force-feed you with plastic meals, rotten movies, and dull in-flight magazines.

The imagination of the apprehensive passenger runs riot

The lack of stimulation unfortunately often allows the imagination of the apprehensive passenger to run riot. Perhaps the crew have died of food-poisoning? Maybe Charlton Heston is even at this moment being winched in through the cockpit window? Wild-eyed hijackers have secretly taken over?

Happily, these things only occur in disaster movies. What is actually happening up front is much more prosaic. The auto-pilot will be flying the aircraft, probably coupled to an automatic navigation system. One pilot will be monitoring this and keeping watch for other aeroplanes, whilst the other handles the radio communications with Air Traffic Control, checks the fuel consumption, and obtains the weather reports for various en-route airfields in case a diversion is needed (passengers occasionally have heart attacks or some other medical problem, and require urgent hospitalisation. We therefore keep tabs on the conditions at airports as we pass them).

Auto-pilot

Usually the autopilot is used extensively on each flight. On modern aeroplanes, the automatic pilot (never, incidentally, called 'George' except by people whose aviation lore began and ended with Biggles) can be engaged about 4 seconds after take-off, and does not have to be disconnected until after the aircraft has landed. (See also Automatic Landing, pages 24 & 25). In between, the autopilot - if it is connected to a navigation computer - will fly the aircraft along the pre-selected route without the need for any further assistance from the crew. That said, most pilots spend at least part of the flight, usually the climb and the latter stages of the descent and landing, flying the aircraft manually - simply because it is such fun!

Of course the crew can override the autopilot at any time, either by disconnecting it completely (usually through a small push-button on the control column), or by leaving it engaged but giving it new instructions.

You're Going to Eat That?

The high point for the crew during this time is when a stewardess produces the meal trays (and yes - we do eat different meals. And the other pilot always gets the better one).

The other pilot always gets the better meal

Engine noise

During cruising flight you may detect the engine noise varying slightly, especially on modern jets with large motors. The reason for these changes is that the engine power is controlled by a computer which is constantly calculating the most economical speed at which to fly. This speed varies slightly in response to the wind, the temperature of the atmosphere, and the weight of the aircraft (which decreases as fuel is used up). Thus the computer from time to time commands small alterations in engine power, and these changes are sometimes audible in the passenger cabin. They are absolutely routine, but are apparently a source of concern to some people.

Other Aircraft - Fellow Travellers

Others worry if they spot another aircraft out of the window. There is no reason why you shouldn't see other aeroplanes: they have every right to be there! However, we pass each other so quickly that, seen sideways on from the passenger cabin, they are usually in sight for only a few seconds, and thus missed unless you happen to be glancing out at just the right time.

Knowing Where We're Going

The world is covered by a network of 'Airways', rather like roadways in the sky, along which civil (and sometimes military) aircraft fly under the watchful eye of Air Traffic Control. These Airways are usually about ten miles wide, and many thousands of feet 'thick'. They run between radio beacons on the ground, which the flight crews use for navigation.

If the flight is over an area with few or no radio beacons (such as deserts, oceans, etc), modern aircraft are equipped with extremely accurate 'inertial navigation' systems. These work on a gyroscopic principle, using either mechanical gyros, or laser-beams whizzing around inside a block of glass. Such 'gyros' are sensitive to the slightest movement, and the aircraft's navigation systems can work out from the resulting outputs such factors as the wind effect, speed over the ground, etc, and since the system knew exactly where we were when we started, it can deduce from all this exactly where we are at any moment during the flight.

An even newer system, based on signals from satellites orbiting the Earth, is now just coming into service. We no longer have to sit in the cockpit running our fingers along a grubby map, or following a ploughed furrow across the desert, as our predecessors did in the old, audacious days.

Airways used to be colour-coded and so had romantic names like Amber 1, Red 19, or Blue 4. Sadly some unimaginative bureaucrat has now decided that they should conform to the international telecommunication alphabet, and so we now have to call them Alpha 1, Romeo 19, Bravo 4 etc.

Within the Airways, flights are separated both vertically and horizontally. The exact spacing depends on how high the aircraft is, whether it is being watched by radar, whether it is arriving at or departing from an airport, etc. But basically, at cruising heights, if the aircraft is being monitored by an Air Traffic Control radar, no other aeroplane is allowed to approach closer than 20 miles if the two flights are at the same height, and within 2000 feet if they are passing one above the other. If no radar is available (for example over oceans or deserts), then the horizontal separation is about 80 miles - roughly ten minutes' flying time. Thus, each aircraft flies within a large, protected 'bubble' of private airspace.

Air Traffic Control

Air Traffic Control tells each flight the route it is to take and the height at which it is to fly, occasionally ordering the pilots to change altitude if the desired separation cannot be maintained. The pilots are in constant radio contact with the Controllers, and are passed from one regional centre to another as the flight progresses. English is used as the standard language of communication anywhere in the world. So although pilots always maintain a good lookout, the main responsibility for keeping aircraft out of each other's way rests with the Air Traffic Controllers.

Contrary to what is often thought, an airliner's radar is not designed to pick up other aircraft. It is there primarily to detect bad weather, and enable the crew to avoid thunderstorms and turbulent cloud. The aircraft's radar can also map the ground to a limited extent, and so is sometimes used as a navigational aid when approaching coastlines, etc. Scientists are currently trying to perfect a system which will alert crews to other potentially conflicting traffic, but it will be some years before such equipment is commonly fitted to airliners.

In the meantime, the present Air Traffic arrangements work very well, and the incidence of 'near misses' is extremely low (although they are usually blown out of all proportion in the popular press on the rare occasions when they do occur). Given, then, that we are all flying along these 'roadways', it is not surprising that you will occasionally see another aeroplane passing by.

Phenomena

At night, we sometimes amuse ourselves on the Flight Deck by flashing our lights in greeting to other voyagers in the dark skies, a harmless diversion that has probably given rise to untold reports of 'flying saucers' by observant citizens on the ground thousands of feet below us.

The white vapour trails which you can sometimes see etched against a blue sky as an airliner flies high overhead are not composed of smoke from the engines, as is sometimes thought. These trails are caused by the hot gasses from the engines' exhaust mixing with the cold atmosphere (typically it is about 57 degrees below zero, centigrade, at the heights at which airliners cruise). Under certain conditions of temperature and humidity, the gasses condense to form 'clouds', the trails which you can see.

Who's Calling?

Meanwhile, back in the passenger cabin, what has the apprehensive flyer found to worry about? What about those electronic 'ding-dongs' that send a stewardess scurrying towards the Flight Deck or cause her to mutter into a telephone? Surely these signals must be harbingers of some developing calamity? Most modern airliners are equipped with a series of electronic chimes, specially devised to madden the passenger who is attempting to doze off. The chimes are of different tones and each has a meaning.

One chime means that the Flight Deck crew are calling - almost always that is just for another cup of coffee, but the

Cabin Crew respond immediately in case the pilots want to pass a message of operational significance. (In a real emergency, most airlines use a pre-arranged coded phrase from the Captain over the Public Address system which alerts the Cabin Crew to the fact that a problem has arisen. In this case the senior member of the Cabin Crew goes immediately to the cockpit to receive instructions).

Another tone means that a passenger has pressed the Steward Call button on his seat or in the panel above his head: he has probably run dangerously low on gin, and the Cabin Crew will respond at once.

Yet another tone means that one of the Cabin Crew is trying to attract the attention of a Steward in another part of the cabin - perhaps to ask for some item which his bar trolley has run out of. This is when you may see the Cabin Crew responding by talking on one of the telephones which are located throughout the cabin of large aeroplanes. There is even a tone which means that someone is stuck in one of the toilets and needs help.

Cruising flight is normally high above any bad weather, and is therefore usually very smooth. However, we occasionally encounter turbulence which causes the aircraft to shudder and rock in a manner which can alarm even the most assured traveller. Turbulence is discussed in detail in the second section of this book.

Getting There

As the flight approaches its destination the Captain will probably come up on the Passenger Address system to tell the passengers that he will shortly be starting the descent, and what the weather is like on the ground. The crew will often switch on the Fasten Seat Belts sign as they begin the descent, not necessarily because they are expecting any turbulence on the way down, but more to give the Cabin Crew time to clear up before the landing, an almost impossible task if people are still milling about in the aisles.

The descent will be marked by a gentle lowering of the aircraft's nose, and the sound of the engine power being reduced. You will also feel your ears beginning to 'pop' as the pressurisation system starts to reduce the altitude in the cabin.

Going Down

Throughout the flight the cabin is pressurised and air-conditioned by air bled from the engines. So whilst the aeroplane itself is cruising at perhaps 35,000 feet, the altitude in the cabin never goes above about 8,000 - roughly the same height as an Alpine ski-resort. However, most airports are much lower than this, so during the descent the pressurisation system gently brings the cabin down to the same height as the airport. Although the aeroplane may be descending much faster, the cabin in which you are sitting will effectively be coming down at around 400 feet per minute, about the same rate as a lift.

It is this reduction in cabin height which causes your ears to 'pop', as air pressure builds up inside them. Most people have no trouble coping with this: yawning, moving your jaws, holding your nose and gently blowing are all effective ways of clearing the ears. The writer has also been told that Sudafed tablets are useful. (Ear plugs, incidentally, are useless). If you have an infant with you, let him or her howl on the way down: a highly efficient way of clearing the ears not readily available to adults.

Problems sometimes occur if people are suffering from heavy colds or sinus infections. In these cases, air trapped in the inner ear passages can cause discomfort or even pain. In extreme cases, it can even lead to a burst ear-drum. Therefore, if you have a heavy cold or sinus trouble, it may be wise to ask a doctor's advice before you fly.

As the aircraft approaches the airport, it will start to slow down. Once again you may hear those whirs and whines as the crew operate the slats and flaps on the wings, and rumbles and clunks as the undercarriage is lowered. The engine noise may also be varying quite noticeably as the pilots change speed and compensate for the extra drag on the aeroplane caused by the extended landing gear and flaps.

'Blind Landing'

At this stage, the pilots are probably being directed by a radar controller towards two narrow electronic beams which are being projected from transmitters close to the runway. One of these beams is aligned with the centreline of the runway. The other is projected upwards at a shallow angle from the threshold of the runway: it defines the correct glide-path to the runway. These two beams are collectively known as an Instrument Landing System (ILS, for short).

The ILS can be picked up by instruments in the cockpit. All the pilots then have to do is follow these beams and they know that the aircraft is properly aligned with the exact centre of the runway, and is coming down on a slope which will bring it over the threshold of the runway at just the right height to make a landing. This can be done either by the pilots flying the aircraft manually and following the indications on their instruments, or automatically by the aeroplane's autopilot. And of course, this can all take place in cloud, mist or fog - the runway itself may not be visible until the very last moments before touchdown.

Most modern aircraft are equipped with automatic landing systems, which means that the aeroplane can carry out the landing in conditions - such as thick fog - in which a human being would be unable to do so. 'Autoland', as it is called, has been around for many years, and it has now reached such a degree of sophistication that the problem nowadays is not one of being able to land and stop on a fog-shrouded runway, it is simply that no-one has yet invented a system of automatic taxying to the terminal building.

The pilot still has to steer the aircraft to the terminal building

The pilot still has to be able to see enough to steer the airliner off the runway after landing and find his way to the airport terminal. For this reason, the minimum visibility in which even an automatic landing can take place is 75 metres. You probably wouldn't feel much like driving home in those conditions anyway, (and you would certainly be infinitely more at hazard on the motorway than you had been in the aeroplane).

The Landing Queue

People sometimes see what appears to be a constant stream of aeroplanes approaching one behind the other to land at a busy airport, and they wonder what happens if you encounter the slipstream of a preceding aircraft. These encounters do sometimes happen, especially on a calm day when there is no wind to help dissipate the aeroplane's wake. However, the Air Traffic Controllers who are arranging the flow of traffic leave a gap of several miles between each aeroplane, the exact amount depending on the relative sizes of the two aircraft (if a small aircraft is following a large one, the separation must be greater). In practice this means that even if we do meet the wake of another aeroplane, it will only be felt as a slight shudder.

Touchdown

Pilots of civilian airliners aim to land about 300 metres along the runway from the threshold, so as to make quite certain that they do not inadvertently touch the ground before the beginning of the tarmac, (grass on the wheels being difficult to explain to the Chief Pilot).

Grass in the wheels is difficult to explain to the Chief Pilot

Landings vary from 'greasers' (so soft you don't even know you're down) to mortifying 'pile-drivers': the latter are very rare, although we've all done them. A typical landing speed for a large jet is around 150 mph.

If you can see the wings, you may notice a series of small 'doors' pop up from the surface just after touch down. These are called 'lift dumpers' and they do just that: they destroy the lift generated by the wing so that all the weight of the aircraft is placed firmly on the wheels, to maximise the effect of braking. (If you notice these 'doors' lifting up in flight, it is because some aircraft use them as a means of assisting turns or slowing down rapidly).

Stopping

The pilots may also use Reverse Thrust on the engines to help slow down the aeroplane on the ground. The shuddering roar from the engines as this happens sometimes worries passengers, who think that something has gone wrong and the pilot is trying to take-off again. Reverse thrust simply saves wear and tear on the brakes and tyres, but in many airlines current practice is not to use it if the landing has taken place on a long runway where there is plenty of room to slow down (it makes a lot of environmentally-unfriendly noise).

'Reverse Thrust' does not mean that the engine actually goes into reverse and 'blows out' of the end which has been 'sucking'. What happens is that when the pilots select reverse thrust in the cockpit, special doors or 'buckets' slide into place, deflecting the engine's exhaust forward at an angle. This is very effective in decelerating the aircraft when it is still travelling fast, but is less efficient as it slows down.

The wheel braking systems themselves are very powerful, and perfectly capable of bringing the aircraft to a stop without the use of reverse thrust from the engines. The braking systems will be at least duplicated and often triplicated, and 'anti-skid' - to prevent the wheels locking, and hence skidding, if too much pressure is applied to the brakes - is virtually standard equipment on all airliners. The most modern aircraft have automatic braking systems, allowing the pilots to preselect a deceleration rate which will be activated on touchdown.

At the end of the landing run, all that remains is to taxi to the parking place or terminal building. As we do so, you will probably hear more 'noises off' as the pilots 'clean up' the aeroplane, retracting the slats and flaps, starting the Auxiliary Power Unit, and so on. When the engines are shut down, you will hear the Cabin Crew leader telling his colleagues over the public address to 'Disarm the slides' or 'Doors to manual' - the signal to the rest of the crew to disable the automatic chutes, so that when the doors are opened the escape slides do not deploy.

The aircraft now becomes the focus of much activity: baggage trucks, catering vehicles, refuellers, engineers, cleaners, and host of others converge on it, all intent on getting it back into the air (and earning its keep) as soon as possible.

So that is it. Yet another routine flight. And now, if perhaps you know a little more about what is going on, a bit less intimidating . . .?

OK. It was all very glib, wasn't it ? If it's as straight-forward as all that WHY DO THE WRETCHED THINGS EVER CRASH? Are you strong enough for Part II, in which that question will be unflinchingly addressed ? If so, read on . . .

PART II

THE CHAMBER OF HORRORS

All those things that really worry you get the cold stare.

Turbulence

Turbulence is what causes an aircraft to shake, shudder, pitch, roll, bucket about and generally behave like a cork in a rough sea. It varies in intensity from the mildest of tremors running through the aeroplane, to extremely unpleasant stomach-churning drops and surges.

The first thing to remember is that, provided you have your seat-belt fastened, it is unlikely that you will come to any harm. This is why sensible passengers keep their seat-belt buckled, even loosely, throughout the flight.

The aeroplane will *not* fall apart, but passengers are sometimes hurt if unexpected turbulence is encountered and they are not strapped in. Then they can be flung out of their seats damaging themselves, fellow passengers, and bits of the expensive machine in which they are travelling.

This doesn't mean that you have to sit lashed tightly to your seat throughout the trip, gripping the armrests, and too terrified even to go to the toilet. But when you *are* in your seat, 'clunk-click'. And if the 'Fasten Seat Belts' sign is on, don't ignore it.

... damaging bits of the expensive machine ...

Turbulence can be caused by various phenomena, but at cruising heights it is most often associated with thunderstorms or very strong winds, called 'Jet Streams'.

The crew use the aircraft's radar to search ahead for thunderstorms and other clouds which might be turbulent, and then it is usually an easy matter to bypass the worst areas.

Clear Air Turbulence

A greater problem is so-called 'Clear Air Turbulence' (CAT), which - as its name implies - occurs in clear air and is thus very difficult to spot in advance. Scientists are trying to develop systems which detect CAT, but these are currently in their infancy. To locate turbulence connected with thunderstorms, the aircraft's radar picks up reflections from raindrops, analyses their size and speed of movement, and can therefore show us where the bumpiest areas are. With CAT, there is nothing for the radar to 'see'.

By studying the weather charts before departure, the crew will know where CAT *may* be found, and other aircraft and Air Traffic Control will broadcast advice alerting flights to known regions of CAT. Then the pilots of aircraft approaching the bumpy region can try various courses of action: they will switch on the 'Fasten Seat Belts' sign, and probably announce over the Public Address that the flight is approaching an area of turbulence. They will slow the aircraft down to a speed at which it will best 'ride' the turbulent air, and they may be able to climb, descend, or alter the route to avoid or reduce the problem.

If we do encounter Clear Air Turbulence, it is often in the vicinity of a 'Jet Stream'. A Jet Stream is a narrow 'tube' of very strong wind, with speeds reaching as high as 200 mph. On a meteorological chart these Jet Streams look rather like snakes writhing around the globe. Of course a Jet Stream can be a Good Thing: if it is going in the same direction as the flight, we can often hitch a free ride in it with no turbulence at all. The turbulence is usually found on the edge of the Jet Stream, rather than actually within it.

If the worst comes to the worst and we do encounter CAT, it will probably not last long: 20 to 30 minutes is typical. It can be extremely uncomfortable for passengers, as the aircraft bucks and heaves, leaving your stomach somewhere up on the roof of the cabin. If you are sitting by a window, you may also see the wings and engines flexing and bobbing about in what may appear to be a most alarming fashion. They are designed to do this: in general, the more flexible the wing, the better the aircraft can ride turbulence. The engine pods, too, nod and sway, absorbing the bumps. Even in the worst turbulence, the screws and rivets which hold everything together won't come loose.

Modern aircraft are incredibly strong. During the very extensive testing which all new types undergo before passengers are allowed to fly in them, it is common for parts of the aeroplane to be 'tested to destruction' in controlled experiments on the ground. If you ever have the chance to see photographs or film of wings undergoing this process, it is an amazing spectacle. The wings are bent upwards by hydraulic jacks until they finally break, but the angle they achieve *before* they fail is quite astonishing: far, far beyond anything they will ever encounter in flight.

To sum up, turbulence is sometimes very unpleasant in the passenger cabin, but it is not going to cause the aeroplane to break up. The crew will be doing everything they can to minimise the discomfort and to find smoother air (turbulence spills *our* coffee, too). During periods of choppiness, which are thankfully rare in the era of high-flying jets, keep your seat belt fastened and think of the experience as being similar to banging your head against a wall - it is lovely when it stops.

Air Pockets

What if we hit an 'Air Pocket'? We won't - there is no such thing. The dropping sensation felt during turbulence is caused by a strong down-draught of air. The bumpiness results from flying from a down-draught into an up-draught, or vice-versa, or when we are being buffeted by gusty winds, as may happen for a few minutes after take-off and before landing on a day when there are gales blowing on the ground.

Bombs and Hijacking

Unfortunately we live in an era in which uninvolved citizens are seen as soft targets by terrorists. This has lead over the last two decades to the introduction of stringent - and often very inconvenient - security measures at airports. These are the first and main line of defence against the bomber and hijacker.

It would not be sensible to detail all the precautions which are taken to prevent terrorists gaining access to aircraft or being in a position to place bombs on board them. Most passengers will be aware of some of them: the screening of hand-baggage, body searches, etc, but other activities are taking place out of sight. These may include the X-raying of all luggage, the presence in the airport of armed and plain-clothes police, the use of State intelligence agencies to pinpoint possible threats, and training given to airline staff to help them recognise the 'personality profile' of potentially unwelcome customers.

Regrettably, the terrorists are becoming more and more sophisticated, and unless the airlines resorted to screening measures which would be intolerable to most passengers, and which would probably cause the entire civil air transport system to seize up, there will always be a very slight risk that a determined, well-equipped group will be able to get a bomb or weapon onto an aircraft.

Even if this happens, the result may not be disastrous. Much experience has been gained in dealing with hijackers, and should an aeroplane be seized, teams of highly skilled negotiators are now available to help defuse the situation. Most airline crews, incidentally, are under strict instructions to comply with a hijacker's demands as far as possible and to refrain at all costs from any 'Action Man' heroics.

This may be tempting fate, but it seems in recent years that a combination of security measures, shifting political fortunes, and a possible change in tactics by potential terrorists has reduced the threat of hijacking to the extent that it should give no more cause for worry than the possibility of being struck by lightning when out for a walk.

If a bomb *does* get aboard an aeroplane it is, of course, extremely serious, but not necessarily catastrophic: many aircraft have survived explosions and landed safely (most famously, perhaps, a BAC 1-11 flown by a certain Far Eastern airline. This aircraft has twice been the chosen venue for attempted suicide by hand grenade. On both occasions the unhappy traveller tried to blow himself up in the rear toilet, successfully achieving his aim, but also ripping a large hole in the cabin roof. On both occasions the aircraft landed with no further problem. The same Captain was flying the aircraft on both occasions).

If a bomb is placed on an aircraft, it will probably be either amongst the baggage in the hold, or in the passenger cabin.

In the former case, if a warning is received in time, the crew will immediately make an emergency descent, depressurize the aircraft (to minimise stresses if the bomb does go off), and land at the nearest airport. The passengers will be told what is happening, and the Cabin Crew will instruct everyone on what to do.

If a suspicious article is found in the cabin, the crew have been trained to deal with it. If possible, the object is moved to the least critical area (usually a door), passengers are moved away from the area, the 'bomb' is packed with blankets and other material which will help absorb any blast, and the pilots descend, depressurize the aeroplane, and divert to a nearby airfield.

Unfortunately, from time to time airlines receive bomb threats from mindless hoaxers. Most companies have a quick-reaction team which analyses the call and decides whether it merits serious consideration. In most cases, the answer is 'no' - it is quite apparent from the tone in which the 'warning' is given that it is some oafish prank.

However, just occasionally there is sufficient doubt to justify further action. If the aircraft is on the ground, this means a thorough search of the aeroplane and its contents, including the passengers' baggage - a very tedious process which involves a long delay. If the aircraft is already in the air when such a threat - known as a 'Specific Threat' - is received, the airline will contact the Captain by radio and advise him. The final decision will be the up to the Captain, but almost invariably he will decide to initiate an immediate diversion, followed by a thorough search of the aircraft - all adding up to a long delay. We are very definitely not amused by hoaxers.

Structural Failure

Passengers sometimes watch as several hundred people clamber aboard one of the big jets. They see tonnes of baggage and cargo being loaded into the holds, and they wonder how an aircraft can carry all that weight. Will the wings come off or the bottom fall out? Will it be able to take-off?

Modern aircraft are both extremely strong and extremely powerful. They are designed to withstand conditions way outside those which they will ever meet during their lifetime (which may be 30 - 40 years). Throughout that life, they are closely monitored by engineers, with the inspections becoming more searching as the aircraft gets older.

Even if it is loaded up to its maximum allowed weight, there is still a wide margin of safety in hand. As we have seen earlier, even at its maximum weight an aircraft must be able to continue with a safe take-off following the failure of one of its engines at the most critical moment.

Both the cabin and floors are very strongly stressed. The cabin floor has to withstand such contingencies as a large lady standing on it in high heels during turbulence - the pressure exerted by a tiny heel in such circumstances can be immense!

The hold floors are equally strong, and careful attention is paid to the loading of the freight and baggage both to ensure that it is evenly distributed and that the correct balance of the aircraft is maintained. Indeed, the captain has to inspect and sign documents to this effect before each flight. (As an aside, we do carry some remarkable cargoes. A few years ago, the writer flew out a holidaymaker who had decided to bring his car with him - a Mercedes. A week later, he decided to send for his other car - a Rolls Royce. Both fitted neatly in our hold).

Doors

Some people may wonder how we know that all the doors are properly closed, including the cargo hold doors which we can't see. All the doors are monitored by micro-switches and linked to an indication in the cockpit. We can thus tell at a glance if everything is properly closed up before we start the engines.

Fuel

Will the aircraft run out of fuel if the winds are stronger than expected, or the flight is delayed?

By law the crew must ensure that before departure sufficient fuel is on board the aircraft to fly to the destination taking into account the expected wind. There must also be enough fuel for the aircraft to make an approach to the destination airport but - for some reason - not be able to land. It must then be able to go to another, alternate airport which the crew have nominated before departure, and to circle overhead *that* airport for 30 minutes before landing. A 'pad' (typically 5%) is then added to all that fuel and the resulting total is the *minimum* which must be on board at departure. Of course, the Captain is perfectly entitled to take as much extra fuel, above this figure, as he wants - even leaving passengers or freight behind if necessary.

Throughout the flight the crew, aided by computer predictions of how the flight should be progressing, keep a very sharp eye on the amount of fuel remaining. If at any point it seems that the reserves are dropping too low, then the crew will divert to an en-route airport for refuelling (a so-called 'Tech Stop').

Since Tech Stops inconvenience passengers and cause the airline extra costs, aircrew prefer to take a conservative view of weather forecasts and route congestion, and load sufficient fuel to preclude any possibility of having to refuel en-route (this is known in the trade as uplifting a bit extra 'for the wife and kids').

Just occasionally, even the best plans turn to worms, as when the flight arrives at its destination to find half the world's airliners are there at the same time, entailing long delays before landing. In this case, the crew will decide to divert to their alternate airport well before the fuel becomes embarrassingly low.

The fuel used by jet aircraft, incidentally, is a form of paraffin. It has a high 'flash point', the temperature at which it will burn. Readers of a certain seniority may remember a dramatic publicity film made by a British airline many years ago, in which the Chairman stood in a puddle of jet aviation fuel, dropping lighted matches into it (and challenging his competitors to do the same with the more volatile fuels which they were, at that time, using). The Chairman remained un-immolated.

Engine Failure

We have seen in the previous section that a single engine failure, even at a critical point during the take-off, is easily manageable. Equally, en-route the failure of an engine - even over a mountain range or in mid-ocean - will have been taken into consideration in advance and the crew will know whether they should continue or turn back. Over the ocean, twin engined aircraft must always be within a specified flying time, on one engine, of a suitable airport.

But supposing *all* the engines fail? This *has* happened. At least twice, Boeing 747 Jumbos have inadvertently flown into clouds of volcanic dust which have clogged up the engines and stopped them. This must have been an extremely frightening experience for all concerned, but on both occasions the crew managed to get several engines working again and made safe landings. There have also been at least two incidents of twin-engined jet airliners having both motors fail. Again, on both occasions, the crew managed to land the aircraft successfully.

The point, however, is that in the almost unimaginable case of all engines failing, everything is *not* lost. Most aeroplanes glide surprisingly well, and - unless the odds were really stacked against you - there would be a very good chance of pulling off a successful (although not necessarily dignified) landing.

Ditching

What if we have to land on water? There have been very few emergency landings on water by modern airliners - 'ditchings' as they are called. There was a successful one in the Caribbean many years ago. But basically there is not enough of a database (thank Goodness!) to be able to give an authoritative answer to this question.

Airliner manufacturers carry out tests with models and computer simulations which offer pilots guidance on the best way to 'ditch' if they should ever have to, and provided the aircraft survives the impact relatively undamaged, they should float quite well.

All flights which approach close to coastlines or will fly over the sea must be equipped with life-jackets for the passengers and crew, and life-rafts if they will spend many hours over water. (In passing, some people take the exhortation that '*Your* lifejacket is under your seat' a bit literally. It is only yours for the duration of the trip. Unlike the in-flight magazine, they are not to be taken home afterwards!).

Fire

A fire in the air is one of the most serious emergencies which a crew can face. There are two potential forms of fire; an engine fire, or a fire in the cabin or cargo hold.

The aircraft is equipped with sensors to detect smoke or heat, and these will immediately alert the crew to any outbreak of fire.

If an engine catches fire, there is only one source which will sustain the flames - the fuel. The fire drill which the crew will carry out cuts off the fuel supply to the engine.

In theory, this alone should put out the fire. But the built-in fire extinguishers will also be discharged. Engine fires are very rare indeed (although dealing with them is regularly practised in the simulator). In older aircraft, with less sophisticated and reliable fire detection systems, false warnings were sometimes an adrenalin-boosting problem, usually caused by a short circuit somewhere in the wiring.

Cabin fires are rarely serious, simply because they are quickly spotted and dealt with. They, too, are thankfully very uncommon, but those which do occur are usually caused by careless smokers dropping cigarettes or accidentally setting something alight. There is always a strict rule against smoking in the toilets, because it is easy for a fire to start if a smoker drops a cigarette into one of the waste-bins there which are full of discarded paper towels.

The toilets are equipped with sensitive smoke detectors: if you are not allowed to smoke in the cabin for any reason, *do not* sneak off to the toilet for a quick drag: the alarm will sound and you will get a richly-deserved roasting from the crew.

The Cabin Crew are thoroughly trained in fighting fires. There are numerous fire extinguishers located around the cabin, and the crew also have special protective and breathing equipment available to enable them to tackle even the most serious blaze.

Modern passenger cabins are extensively fire-proofed; the seats and their covers, the carpets etc will be at least fire-retard-ant, and research is being carried out continuously to improve the fire-proof qualities of all the materials and furnishings.

There has been some talk of equipping aircraft with 'smoke hoods' for the passengers, which could be donned if a fire breaks out and the cabin fills with fumes. These give the head some protection, and a built-in air supply enables the wearer to breath even in a heavily contaminated atmosphere. However, current opinion amongst the aviation safety regulatory bodies is that these things are of limited use: untrained persons find them hard to put on, and there is also a risk that they engender a false sense of security and impede the speed at which an aircraft can be evacuated.

Other work is being carried out on 'water-mist' systems. These consist of nozzles spraying a fine mist of water into the cabin in the event of a fire or accident, and have been shown to be remarkably successful in containing fire, smoke, and heat. However, major problems remain to be overcome before they are fitted to airliners, not least being to ensure that they cannot be discharged inadvertently: a few score soggy passengers is one thing, but the effect an unwanted deluge might have on the aircraft's delicate electronics is another.

Fires in aircraft cargo holds can be disastrous, and several fatal accidents have resulted from such incidents. The main line of defence against cargo hold fires is preventing hazardous items getting onto the aircraft in the first place. There is a long list of restricted items which cannot be carried on passenger flights, or which must be specially packed if they are to be flown.

Anyone sending freight by air is required to sign declarations stating what their consignment consists of - with very severe penalties for any cheating. Airline freight personnel check packages carefully for any signs of damage before they are loaded.

It is less easy to control what passengers put in their suitcases. Did YOU know, for example, that you should not carry mercury thermometers or barometers? If they break, even tiny amounts of mercury can react with the metal skin of the aircraft and cause immense damage. Or non-safety matches which can ignite spontaneously and cause a fire in your suitcase, which can then spread to other baggage and freight?

If a fire does break out in a cargo hold or amongst the baggage, it will be detected by sensors in those areas. The holds themselves are usually either airtight, so any fire will quickly be starved of oxygen and go out, or they will be equipped with fire extinguishers which can be discharged from the cockpit.

How Do Aeroplanes Fly?

If you hold a piece of paper horizontally in front of you with the thumb and fore-finger of each hand, the end the furthest away from you will droop down. If you now blow gently over the curve thus formed, the paper will lift up. This is why aeroplanes fly.

The wings of an aircraft are shaped rather like the drooping piece of paper: the upper surface is curved - more towards the front than the back - whilst the lower surface is flat. As the wing is pushed along (the function of the engines) the air passing over the upper surface has to move faster than the air going underneath, because it has further to go. This creates a lower pressure above the wing than below, and hence the wing is 'sucked' upwards, a process called 'lift'.

In order to turn, the wings must be tilted (merely moving the rudder at the back would cause the aircraft to 'skid' round corners in a most uncomfortable manner). So turning is achieved through the use of ailerons, small flaps on the rear of each wing which move in opposite directions on each side of the aircraft. These effectively alter the curvature of the wing to which they are attached and so one wing moves up and the other down, creating a 'banked' condition. The 'lift' is now not only working directly upwards, to overcome gravity, it is also pulling the aeroplane left or right.

This is a pretty simplistic explanation of what is going on and the writer won't entertain any correspondence from outraged aerodynamicists. It applies to most types of aeroplane except Concorde and helicopters. Concorde wings work on a principle of digitally-enhanced macrobiotic vortices or something similar. Don't even *try* to understand how it flies: merely pay your money and feel privileged to sit in one of the most beautiful pieces of technology ever to rattle your windows. Helicopters are something else (see below).

(Just as an aside, in one of his earlier professional exams, the writer was asked to describe the aerodynamic process by which an aircraft turns. Re-reading his solution just before 'time up', he found that he had conclusively and scientifically proved that it is absolutely impossible for an aeroplane to turn. He passed the exam).

Stalling

'Stalling' is what happens if an aeroplane flies too slowly or too fast, so that the airflow over the wings becomes so seriously disrupted that they can no longer provide the lift to keep the aeroplane airborne. At this stage, the machine takes on many of the flying characteristics of a brick.

Pilots take great care to ensure that the aircraft never comes anywhere near to these upper or lower limits of the 'flight envelope'. In modern aeroplanes, there are a variety of devices and warnings to prompt the crew to the fact that they are approaching a stalled condition. In fact, the very latest aircraft (for example the 'fly-by-wire' Airbus 320, 330, and 340) are 'stall-proof': their computers will ultimately override any input from the pilots which could lead to the aircraft becoming stalled.

On take-off and landing the aeroplane will be flying at about

25-30% above the stalling speed, with a similar margin below the 'high speed stall' being maintained during the cruise.

Even in the extremely unlikely event that the aircraft does, somehow, get into a stall, the recovery from it is quick and easy (and another of the manoeuvres which are practised in the simulator).

Helicopters

You're not really going to fly in one of these, are you?
As you approach a helicopter, you will notice that it doesn't have any wings. This should put you on your guard. Instead, it has those spindly, flimsy-looking things attached to the top. They are called rotors, and the theory is that if you whirl them around fast enough, the entire contraption will rise into the air and stay there. The closer you get to a helicopter, the less credible this idea seems.

Helicopter pilots have much in common with Mr Uri Geller and those chaps who saw their assistants in half on stage. Helicopter flying is, in fact, an extraordinary optical illusion. The fact that it seems to be a very safe form of aerial travel merely reinforces this observation.

The Crew

'How do I know if they're any good?' The writer's natural modesty makes this an awkward topic, so let's look at it purely factually.

To be a pilot you do NOT have to be a superman (just good-looking, charming, etc . . .) You need a reasonable standard of education and health, good coordination, and a certain mental outlook. The rest is training.

Civilian pilots obtain their training in different ways. Some come from a military flying background, while others are the product of the civilian training system. This latter is very expensive: it now costs someone embarking on a flying career about £65,000 to obtain the basic licence which will allow them to fly 'for hire and reward'. The course which leads to this licence lasts about a year at a flying school approved by the Civil Aviation Authority.

The course involves a study of all aspects of aviation, including aerodynamics, thermodynamics, meteorology, radio, law, and a host of other subjects. At the same time, the student will be undergoing flying instruction, progressing from simple single engine aircraft, to twin-engine aeroplanes with more sophisticated instruments, which he or she must learn to fly without looking out of the cockpit. The culmination of the course is a series of flying and written exams, in which the pass mark is very high.

Of course many would-be pilots can't afford such a course, and either can't get into, or don't want to join the military. If they are very lucky, they may find an airline to sponsor their training, in return for a certain minimum number of years service for that company. But others will have to embark on the sheer hard graft of the 'self-improver' route: getting a Private Pilot's licence (costing several thousand pounds, this licence only allows you to fly for pleasure, not for remuneration), then scraping together enough hours of flying to become an instructor (and getting paid at last, albeit often only a pittance). Working thus, the pilot will build up his experience until he or she reaches the minimum required to be allowed to take the examinations for a Commercial Pilot's Licence (CPL).

A CPL allows someone to act as a co-pilot on a large aeroplane like an airliner. He or she will be fully qualified to fly the aeroplane, and in routine airline operations the captain and the co-pilot take it in turns to do the take-off and the landing, (although if the weather is bad or the flying is likely to be particularly demanding, the captain will take over). So a co-pilot is, in effect, undergoing an 'apprenticeship' - he or she is a 'captain in waiting'.

To qualify for the licence which allows you to be a captain requires years' more experience and the passing of yet more exams. After that, the airline itself will set stringent standards for aspiring commanders: it isn't about to entrust just anyone with millions of dollars-worth of hardware and customers. The route to a civil aviation command is long and hard.

Few other professions are as rigorously checked as that of a pilot. As we have seen earlier, each individual typically undergoes at least seven medical or competency checks each year, all of which must be passed.

The medicals become more searching as you get older, and include sight, hearing, and cardiac checks. After the age of 60 we are no longer allowed to fly in command of a heavy aircraft, a definition which includes most airliners.

The competency checks are carried out by the Cruel and Sadistic Instructors referred to earlier, (they are known to their faces as Check Pilots or Training Captains, or Sir).

At least once per year each pilot will find a Training Captain sitting in on a routine flight, observing the captain's or co-pilot's performance. These are comparatively 'friendly' events, since the presence of witnesses (passengers) tempers the Training Captain's more barbaric instincts. He is really waiting to get his victims into the 'simulator'.

'Simulators' are exact reproductions of the aircraft's cockpit which are mounted on hydraulically-operated legs (to impart a sense of motion). The whole contraption is controlled by computers, and the most modern versions are equipped with sophisticated visual systems (so that you can 'see' through the windscreens), and are capable of reproducing the flying characteristics of a real aeroplane with uncanny accuracy.

They could be fun, like some giant arcade game, but they're not: they are equipped with a station at which the Cruel and Sadistic Instructor sits, confronted by buttons allowing him to introduce an almost infinite variety of catastrophes into the proceedings. A simulator in the hands of a CSI is, quite simply, a high tech version of a medieval torture chamber. An airline pilot typically has to undergo at least four sessions in this device each year.

A typical simulator 'ride' starts with a fire and engine failure on take-off from a runway which (of course) is shrouded in fog (thus making a quick return to land difficult or impossible). Thereafter things progress rapidly from bad to worse. Needless to say, the autopilot isn't working and the co-pilot will have been told to display the maximum level of incompetence of which he is capable. A simulator session goes on for about three or four hours, which is probably contrary to the Geneva Convention.

The CSI, of course, hugely enjoys all this. When not engaged in pressing buttons to heap further disasters upon the wilting shoulders of the wretched victim, he will be making copious notes for use at the de-briefing session which rounds the whole thing off (this, in itself, makes the average Interrogation Centre seem like a Charm School).

Amazingly, most pilots recuperate from this bestial treatment surprisingly quickly - often by the second round in the bar afterwards. By the third round, many even begin to feel that it has been a Good Thing: if they can handle *that*, then anything which goes wrong in real life should be plain sailing.

Is there a safest place to sit in an aircraft?

There is a popular myth that sitting at the rear of aircraft is safer than sitting in the front. The UK's Civil Aviation Authority is not aware of any statistical evidence showing this to be the case, although the Flight Data Recorder - the so-called 'Black Box' (actually it is usually a red ball) is often located in the tail section.

If you do sit in the rear, the down-side is that this is often the smoking section (you are much more likely to die of smoking-related problems than in an aircrash), and the rear of some aircraft tend to sway more uncomfortably than the front end in turbulence. It may also be noisier at the back, especially in rear-engined types.

Large, wide-bodied aircraft seem to offer better chances of survival in an accident, perhaps because they have a lot of 'structure' to absorb impact forces.

If it makes you feel better, you can check in early and ask to be seated in one of the rows adjacent to an emergency exit (these also have the added bonus of extra legroom). These rows are generally restricted to able-bodied passengers.

The most important contribution you can make to your safety when in an aircraft is to notice where the emergency exits are (not just the door by which you entered the aeroplane), and pay attention to the Cabin Crew's pre-take off safety briefing. In the extremely unlikely event of anything going wrong, don't panic, and do exactly as you are told by the crew without delay. If the accident is survivable, your chances of getting out are very high provided you keep calm, know what to do, and follow instructions.

Which are the safest airlines?

You pay for the libel lawyer, and I'll tell you which airlines I would avoid! In fact, most airlines that you are likely to consider in your travel plans are OK. European and North American airlines generally maintain a high standard. Size is not necessarily an indication of quality: many small airlines operate to very high standards. Of all international airlines, those based in Australia have maintained an exceptionally good record over a very long time.

It may be best to avoid airlines which are known to be in financial difficulty (although the last thing they will want is an accident to add to their problems). You might also want to choose an airline which operates modern equipment: ask your travel agent what kind of aircraft the airline flies.

Despite the occasional screaming headline in the tabloid press, there are no 'rogue' aircraft types. All airliners are exhaustively tested before they receive government approval to carry passengers.

Charter airlines should not be seen as less safe than scheduled carriers.

'Delay due to technical reasons.' What does this really mean?

This is the 'catch-all' excuse airlines often use to cover a delay, without perhaps realising the distress this can cause to an apprehensive passenger. It can cover everything from a major breakdown in one of the aircraft's systems, to the fact that the pilot has had a puncture on his way to the airport. It is a very irritating excuse; just marginally better than being given no reason at all for a delay.

The most important thing to remember is that if the aeroplane needs fixing it *will* be fixed before you fly in it. The crew have families, too, and will know more about the extent of the problem than you do, as you sit frustratedly in the departure lounge. The crew will not be fobbed off with anything less than a fully flyable aircraft.

However, on those rare occasions when a system defect appears shortly before departure, the main problem can be in determining how long it will take to fix. The engineers first have to locate the source of the trouble and then do something about it. If something isn't working as it should, the cause may not be immediately apparent: it may simply be a case of plugging in a replacement 'black box', or it may require the removal of lots of bits to get at the offending part. Engineers are very loathe to commit themselves until they are sure of what they are up against, and this lack of 'hard' information to pass to waiting passengers is often a cause of much frustration.

Can the passengers 'un-balance' an aircraft by walking around?

No. Very occasionally we ask passengers to sit in particular seat rows to optimise the balance of the aircraft for take-off, but once we are airborne there is no problem. The aircraft's trimming system is very powerful (it moves the entire 'horizontal stabiliser', the small 'wings' at the back of the aircraft), so there is no way that even such phenomena as a queue for the toilet or people walking up and down could affect the aeroplane's balance.

Why do aeroplanes tilt when they turn?

In order to turn, aeroplanes must tilt, so that part of the lift being generated by the wings is used as a turning force (see also above: Why do aeroplanes fly?). In civil flying, the degree of tilt - known as 'bank' - is usually very little, always less than thirty degrees from the horizontal (although it can look a lot more).

As the aircraft banks, it produces various effects which may be noticeable to those on board. Banking increases the amount of 'drag' on the aircraft - the degree of resistance to the air. This means that to maintain speed, the engine power must be increased. You may hear a slight change in engine note as the aeroplane turns.

The centrifugal forces created during a turn make you slightly 'heavier'. In the gentle turns practised on airliners, this is scarcely noticeable, but a military pilot turning hard in a jet fighter may find his weight shooting up eight or nine times.

'I am not in control'

This is a very common reaction amongst apprehensive flyers. Probably the best way of coming to terms with this feeling is to take a philosophical approach and perhaps read the paragraph above on Crew. An airline crew is very highly trained and you are in good hands. You probably do not worry too much about being in a train or bus, although you are not in control of these forms of transport either, (and far less money will have been spent on training the crew and servicing the vehicle).

'Once I'm in the aeroplane I can't get out'

Civil airliners do not carry parachutes: for a start, we cannot open the doors in flight (the air pressure inside the cabin makes this impossible, even if the door mechanism was operated) and anyway it is highly unlikely that untrained passengers could make a successful parachute descent even if they had time to put on parachutes in an emergency and could 'bail out'. So although you cannot get out, you are in a very safe 'cocoon' whilst you are on board.

Computers - can they go wrong?

As the enlightened reader will realise, there is no such thing as an <u>in</u>animate object. Everything has a character of its own, usually malevolent. There is no better example of this truism than computers, as anyone knows who owns a PC and has watched an entire morning's work disappear from the screen simply because you have inadvertently pressed the wrong button. Can the same thing happen with all this wizardry aboard the aircraft?

Great care is taken to prevent any such catastrophe, first of all by ensuring that the weakest link - the pilots - cannot get access to the software programmes (the stuff that makes the computers work). These programmes are designed, produced and tested in places called Silicon Valleys by people of mind-boggling intellect, who are not supposed to goof-off on the job. It is the task of those Right Stuff manufacturers' test pilots to ensure that these programmes really are error-free during the prolonged trials which take place before an aircraft enters service.

Most of the computers on board, especially the most vital ones, also check themselves and will let the crew know if they are not happy with what they find. For example, the programmes of the flight control computers in the latest generation of 'fly-by-wire' airliners are written in different languages by different companies (which are not allowed to communicate with each other). The computers then check that these programmes match *exactly* before they execute the resulting commands. It is thus highly unlikely that a serious error could be duplicated within this system.

Ultimately, of course, there is always that little red button on the control column which, if pressed, cuts out virtually all the automatics and leaves the pilots in full control. Computers *hate* that little button, and its mere existence is usually enough to keep them in line.

Are there any simple ideas which would make flying safer?

There are some things which could be introduced which probably would make flying safer.

Fitting retractable 'lap and diagonal' seat belts would offer much better protection in the event of an accident than the simple lap straps which are currently used (rear-facing seats would be even better, but are strongly resisted by passengers). Why aren't they fitted? Because the first airline to do so would risk giving the impression that it was less safe than its competitors.

Strengthening overhead lockers would help to prevent them coming loose in an accident. This area is being worked on by aircraft manufacturers and government air safety organisations.

Establishing Duty Free facilities on *arrival,* rather than on departure, would prevent hundreds of potential 'fragmentation and incendiary' devices (bottles of spirits) being brought on board every flight. Some enlightened airports already practice this; why don't they all?

So why do they crash?

Before we look at why mishaps occur, let's get the accident rate in context. Far too often lurid tabloid headlines following an accident obscure the fact that such events are extraordinarily remote.

For much of the following information, I am indebted to Flight International, the world's leading aviation magazine.

The world's airlines make about one million flights each month, carrying over 1,125 <u>million</u> passengers annually. Over the last decade there have been about 44 fatal airline accidents each year, in which just over 1000 people die. But during this period, the number of flights has risen by 42% and the number of passengers travelling is up by 50%, so in real terms aviation safety continues to improve from year to year.

This is an extremely good record by any standards (although you will find no complacency in the flying world). Your chances of being involved in an accident when you board an aircraft are very, very small indeed.

As a comparison, about 80,000 people are killed on the roads of Europe each year.

Why are there any aircraft accidents at all?

Statistically, the main cause remains human error. Although manufacturers are continually making airliners easier and safer to fly and maintain, whilst human beings are involved in the chain, from design to manufacturing to maintenance to flying, errors will occasionally creep in. Most often these are of little consequence: just very occasionally, they are catastrophic.

You can minimise your exposure to such errors by flying with airlines which enjoy a sound reputation and which fly modern, well-equipped and well-maintained aircraft. Most 'western' airlines fall into this category, but so do many from so-called 'Third World' countries (which is why the <u>world-wide</u> accident rate is so low).

Typically about 65% of accidents are put down to 'human error', although in the past this has sometimes been used as a convenient 'catch-all' term through which blame can be pinned on a 'scapegoat', whilst strongly contributory errors of omission and commission remain obscured.

In recent years, increasing attention has been paid to the interface between man and machine, 'Human Factors', and 'Crew Resource Management' (HF and CRM). Or in plain language: 'why does the Right Stuff sometimes turn out to be the Wrong Stuff?' Much of the thrust to improve flight safety now involves psychology, with crews learning how to interact and communicate better, and to recognise developing situations which could lead to problems.

Accidents almost always result from a chain of events, which may start quite innocuously. If the chain can be broken at almost any point, the accident will be averted.

Although some dyed-in-the-wool aviators dismiss all this as 'psycho-babble', hard evidence shows that crews which have received this form of training perform better than those which have not. (Dr Georgiou, who wrote Part III of this book, is a leader in this field of aviation psychology and has been running Human Factors and Crew Resource Management courses of his own design for several years).

The next main cause of fatal accidents (about 37%) is 'Controlled Flight into Terrain' (CFIT) - the flight of a perfectly serviceable aircraft into the ground. Very often this involves at least some degree of human error, and Human Factors and CRM training seem likely to bring about marked improvements in this area.

Human error and CFIT are followed by 'weather' and 'technical failure' in the league of causes of accidents. Hijacking and sabotage account for a tiny proportion of incidents (for example, in a recent year the 5 deaths attributed to hijacking were all of the terrorists themselves).

Flying can never be 100% safe (nor indeed can anything else. Life itself has, after all, been described as a 'terminal condition'). However, as I hope this book has shown, you are probably safer in an aeroplane than when undertaking almost any other activity.

PART III

Conquering Your Fear The Natural Way

by

Dr George Georgiou

Introduction

Perhaps one of the things that flyers fear most is having an anxiety attack. This is where their level of anxiety and tension reaches such a high level that often there is the feeling that the end is near. Nothing can be further from the truth! I therefore believe that it is very important for anyone who suffers from anxiety or phobias to understand fully what is happening to them during an anxiety attack. Understanding the symptoms is the first step to being able to combat them.

Many people who have anxiety attacks feel that they are in impending danger and fear dying of a heart attack, a stroke, or some other wicked ailment. The reason for this is that the subjective feelings of anxiety, particularly at their peak, are so frightening and awesome that anyone would feel like death is knocking on their door. Gaining a detailed understanding of what is happening to your mind and body during an anxiety attack will facilitate your ability to control the situation. It will also help put into perspective those distorted feelings of impending danger that surface, hence alleviating the intensity of the attack.

In the following pages I hope to be able to explain in simple terms what anxiety is, what are its symptoms, and what are some of the ways of coping with it, which include psychological methods of relaxation, the relevance of diet and nutrition, and some 'natural tranquilisers' that can be taken. I have basically tried to think of things that can be easily implemented or taken whilst on-board the aircraft.

I think it is also important to clarify from the very beginning that anxiety, however acute, CANNOT, and WILL NOT kill you! There is absolutely no way that an anxiety attack can do any serious physical harm to the body. It can certainly make you feel extremely uncomfortable and fearful, but on a physical level it can do nothing harmful.

Most of the feelings and sensations that we have during an anxiety attack are due to the stimulation of part of the nervous system called the Autonomic Nervous System. There are two parts to this system, the Sympathetic part which basically switches the body 'on' and prepares it to deal with any perceived danger, real or otherwise, and the Parasympathetic part which basically switches the body 'off' and brings it back to its normal state. Immediately after an anxiety attack, which usually lasts a few minutes (although it often feels like it is lasting for hours), the Parasympathetic part of the Autonomic Nervous System is triggered and returns the body back to its normal state. So let us look in brief how and why your body reacts when it is turned 'on' and is in a state of anxious turmoil.

ANXIETY: The Dreaded Enemy

A public speaker who goes on stage and cannot utter a word because his mind has gone blank.

An accomplished pianist finds that his fingers have gone stiff as he begins playing at an international concert.

An intelligent student taking an exam cannot think or write as her mind is streaming with irrelevant thoughts.

Each of these mishaps is characteristic of the condition commonly called anxiety. One of the paradoxical features of acute anxiety is that the person seems to bring on unwittingly what he fears or detests the most. In fact, the greater the fear of a specific situation or event, the more likely it seems to the sufferer that it will actually happen.

To understand how the anxiety reaction seems to produce just those things that an individual most abhors, reflect on this report by a college professor with fears of public speaking:

'As I stand talking to the audience, I hope that my mind and voice will function properly, that I won't lose my balance, and everything else will function. But then my heart starts to pound, I feel pressure build up in my chest as though I'm ready to explode, my tongue feels thick and heavy, my mind feels foggy and then goes blank. I can't remember what I have just said or what I am supposed to say. Then I start to choke. I can barely push the words out. My body is swaying; my hands tremble. I start to sweat and I am ready to topple off the platform. I feel terrified and I think that I will probably disgrace myself.' (Beck and Emery, 1985).

We can see from this passage that there are various components of anxiety, namely: (1) a physiological reaction of sweating, increased heart rate and dizziness; (2) various negative thoughts (cognitions) such as 'I am going to disgrace myself'; (3) a wish to avoid the anxiety-provoking situation; (4) feelings (emotions) of terror and calamity; (5) behavioural changes such as losing balance or not being able to speak.

PHOBIAS: Anxiety at its Worst

Phobia refers to a specific kind of fear and is defined as 'an unreasonable fear of a particular object or situation'. The key phrase is 'unreasonable fear,' as everyone has fears of certain things. A person confronted by a venomous rattle snake will undoubtedly be afraid, and justifiably so. However, a person faced with a small, harmless grass snake or slow-worm has no need to be overtly afraid and anxious. A phobia is characterised by an intense desire to avoid the feared situation, and evokes anxiety when one is exposed to that situation.

Next to alcohol abuse, phobias are the most common psychological disorders. In hierarchical order, fear of snakes comes top of the list, followed by fear of heights, fear of mice, and then fear of flying, commonly called Aerophobia. Approximately 20% of people are afraid of flying, but it is only a small percentage of these that find the fear so incapacitating that they avoid flying altogether. Such people will probably not be reading this little book!

People who tend to react with violent anxiety before and during an aeroplane trip are probably the ones who will avoid flying at all costs. Some fear they will suffocate on the aeroplane due to deprivation of air as a result of interference with the air supply. Others are afraid that their tension will build to a level where they will lose control of themselves. More commonly, however, the phobic flyer fears the aeroplane will crash and that he will be killed, even though flying is one of the safest forms of transport.

Some individuals begin thinking of disaster when they hear any change in engine rhythm or vibration, or when the plane enters cloud or turbulence, or even when they see the stewardess hurrying down the cabin. This is why it is important to read the first part of this book, as my experienced co-author, Captain Adrian Akers-Douglas, explains all the technical aspects of flying in simple, succinct detail. This is an excellent starting point for alleviating anxiety.

Other people who fear air travel are concerned about loss of control in social situations. They may be afraid that they will vomit or faint in the aeroplane and subsequently suffer humiliation. Finally, a significant proportion of aeroplane phobias are related to agoraphobia, where there is a combination of the fear of being trapped in a closed space and the fear of being separated from a loved one who cares for us and would take care of us whatever may happen.

PHOBIC SYMPTOMS: How does the body cope?

According to Beck and Emery (1985), the symptoms of anxiety tend to trigger many different reactions in the body; psychological, emotional, behavioural and physiological. Some of the psychological (cognitive) symptoms may include (presented in hierarchical order of significance):

- Difficulty in concentration
- Fear of losing control
- Fear of being rejected
- Inability to control thinking
- Confusion
- Mind blurred
- Inability to recall important things
- Sentences broken or disconnected
- Blocking in speech
- Fear of dying
- Stuttering

It is important to note the person's fear of injury or death - however unlikely this may be in reality. It is usually this fear that causes the anxiety which generates the physical symptoms, which in turn feeds the fear that you are going to have a heart attack or stroke or whatever. **It is only a fear** - you are **not** going to have a heart attack or die. It requires much more than anxiety to kill us!

The person who suffers from anxiety and phobia is indulging in faulty thinking. Typically, they 'catastrophize' - dwelling on the worst possible outcome of a situation. The anxious person usually exaggerates the possible consequences of an event. An example of this behaviour would be a preoccupation with the possibility of the aeroplane crashing and of being killed. The chance of this happening is one in millions, since flying is such an extraordinarily safe way of travelling - in commercial aviation there are about 1.3 accidents for each one million flying hours! The chances of having an accident on the road are far, far higher.

Apart from faulty thinking, perhaps the most frightening aspect of the panic attack is the loss of control that the individual has always taken for granted. He has to struggle to retain or regain voluntary control over focusing, concentration, attention, and action. At times, the difficulty in focusing extends to a sense that he is losing consciousness, although actual loss of consciousness is rare.

Of course, the most striking characteristic of the panic attack is the feeling of being engulfed by uncontrollable anxiety. This feeling has been described by many of my patients as 'unending pain' and 'the worst experience of my life - I thought I was going to die!'

Apart from psychological symptoms, there are various emotions (affective) involved too, such as:

Fearful/terrified	*Impatient*	*Frightened/scared*
Nervous/anxious	*Edgy*	*Jittery/jumpy*
Tense/wound up	*Alarmed/scared*	*Uneasy*

The emotional or affective symptoms are often the most dramatic and may vary from edginess and tension to terror, and are usually those that make the person feel very unwell.

The behavioural symptoms generally reflect either the hyperactivity of the behavioural system or else its inhibition. Some of the behavioural symptoms include:

Avoidance	*Speech problems*
Impaired coordination	*Restlessness*
Quick breathing (hyperventilation)	*Inhibition*
Fleeing	*Postural collapse*

Generally, there will be an increase in muscular activity even when sitting. This may show itself in grimacing, by continual movements of hands and often by the rest of the body, and by chain smoking, sighing, shaking, tremors, and pacing back and forth.

The physiological symptoms reflect a readiness of the total organism for self-protection. Some of these physiological symptoms (physical) include:

Palpitations	*Faintness*
Shortness of breath	*Insomnia*
Tremors	*Clumsy motions*
Abdominal pain	*Nausea*
Pressure to urinate	*'Hot and Cold' spells*

The body generally prepares itself for the 'flight or fight' reaction which characterises phobic anxiety states. The heart and cardiovascular system will therefore increase their output to provide more blood to the muscles and other organs, the pupils dilate, the gut slows down, etc.

These bodily sensations are often 'catastrophized' by the anxious person. Thus:

Symptom:	Interpreted as:
Abdominal or chest pain & faintness	Heart attack!
Changes in mental functioning (difficulty in focusing, 'fogginess', depersonalisation, etc)	Going mad!
Difficulty in catching breath	'I will stop breathing and die!'
Faintness	Impending coma and death!
Generalised sense of loss of control over internal sensations	Uncontrollable or bizarre behaviour!

It is again important to realise that these uncomfortable and painful symptoms **cannot** cause heart attacks, strokes, madness, apnoea (stopping breathing) or total loss of control. At worst they will make you feel extremely uncomfortable and agitated, and you will not be able to keep focused and concentrated on any one task. But that is all!

COPING TECHNIQUES: What can you do about your anxiety?

Today there are many techniques used by scientists to deal with the dreaded symptoms of anxiety. There are psychological techniques which focus on changing the way that the person perceives his anxiety (cognitive therapies), the way a person feels about the perceived threat (affective therapies) and the way a person behaves (behavioural therapies).

There is also another natural approach which is of particular interest to me as a biologist, nutritionist and natural therapist, and this is the natural, alternative approach. This involves using a variety of nutritional supplements such as vitamins, amino acids and minerals, combined with an adequate diet to help control and alleviate anxiety symptoms. One can also use the Bach Flower Remedies, which I will discuss in more detail later.

Although this is a huge subject which could fill many volumes, let me outline here a few techniques which can be used by an anxious person sitting on the seat of an aeroplane. These include doing easy relaxation exercises, using positive images to replace negative and frightening ones, and possibly using a variety of nutritional supplements and Bach Flower Remedies which can help a person relax. Let us begin by examining a simple technique that can be used from the comfort of your seat for changing and modifying those negative images which spark a lot of the anxiety.

POSITIVE IMAGERY - think positive, feel positive

For a long time now psychologists have realised that undesirable visual images often stimulate negative thoughts, which in turn provoke anxiety and tension. Thinking that the plane will fall any minute due to an engine failure or some other mechanical problem is bound to make you feel tense and anxious. The opposite is also true; if we can focus on pleasant, positive images (sunbathing, being with our favourite partner, being loved by a friend or relative), then this will tend to create more positive thoughts and maintain a state of inner relaxation. The identification of this cognitive process is a positive step forward towards gaining mastery of your phobic anxiety.

For example, suppose you are beginning to have negative thoughts about the aeroplane crashing. You can see this clearly on your mind's 'television' screen. What you must try to do is to change the channel. Flick the internal 'switch' and select a more appropriate programme.

Close your eyes and try to tune into your breathing. If you are breathing too fast, slow down and take a few slow deep breaths. Now try to focus on a soothing scene -

- Sunbathing on a beautiful tropical beach with the sun's rays passing over your body and sapping the anxiety and tension out of your feet.

- Or you can imagine walking through a picturesque green forest with the one you love, really enjoying the wonderful warmth of the moment.

You can think of absolutely anything that captures your fantasy and imagination and makes you feel good. It may be making love to your best partner, or eating your favourite food, or whatever. Let me try to spin a pleasant fantasy that you can dwell on for a few minutes. I suggest that you read the following carefully, and then close your eyes, rest back in your seat, make yourself warm and comfortable, and fantasise away:

Imagine yourself lying comfortably on a golden, sandy beach. It is late afternoon and the sun is warm but not scorching. The beach is quiet with very few people to disturb you. There are a couple of children quietly playing volleyball, and a young couple next to you really enjoying each other's company. You can feel the sun's heat penetrating your body deeply and soothing those tense and aching muscles. You can feel the heat entering your head through your nose and slowly sifting through you until it exits through your feet, taking away all the tensions. You are really relaxed and enjoying the comfortable state of being at peace with yourself. You can hear the rush of the waves in rhythm with your breathing, deep and slow. You can hear the cry of the seagulls hovering above a small fishing trawler, and the sounds of the children playing

volleyball. You can hear all these sounds, but they are in the background, far from your immediate concentration. Lie on the beach in a state of deep relaxation and inner peace for a couple of hours. Enjoy the total peace of mind.

Now you try it! Make yourself as comfortable as possible on your seat, take a few good, deep breaths, and begin conjuring up this positive image. As you get more experienced, you can change the image to one you like better. It is difficult to have a positive image in mind, whilst concomitantly having a negative one too. So the more positive images you have, the more relaxed you will be.

BREATHING CORRECTLY - fundamental to relaxation

Strangely, many of us do not breath correctly. This can cause much discomfort, ill health and a feeling of distress. People often use their chest alone when breathing; but it is equally important to use the abdomen too. When we use the abdomen, we fill **all** of our lungs, including the little alveoli (air sacs) right at the bottom of our lungs. A part of dealing with anxiety is to change our breathing patterns.

Anxiety and tension lead to rapid and deep breathing, which is called hyperventilation. This flushes out too much carbon dioxide from the lungs, making the body more alkaline than normal. Breathing like this can cause many of the symptoms of anxiety, so we get trapped in a vicious circle of cause and effect. So, are **you** breathing correctly? Try the following:

Get into a comfortable sitting position, place one hand on your abdomen. Breathe slowly through your nose, while keeping your mouth closed. Take slow gentle breaths. As you inhale push your abdomen out against your hand - feel your abdomen expand and your hand rise. Hold for two seconds and then exhale slowly through your nose. Feel your stomach deflate and your hand fall. Repeat four times.

As you master this exercise, you will be able to do it without positioning your hands on your abdomen. Concentrating on the abdominal movements will slowly help to correct faulty breathing patterns. I recommend that you practice this about 3-4 times per hour, throughout the whole flight. It only takes seconds to do, and could be an important link to breaking the anxiety chain that has developed.

QUIETING REFLEX (QR)

Another easy relaxation technique that has been explained by Dr. Terry Looker and Dr. Olga Gregson in their book on stress is called the Quieting Reflex. It is very simple, and only takes a few seconds to implement, but can have excellent results in the alleviation of anxiety and tension. You try it!

Close your eyes. Pinpoint in your mind what is annoying or stressing you. Say to yourself slowly, 'Relax, relax. I'm not going to let this get to me.'

Smile to yourself. You can practice smiling to yourself without showing a smile on your face. Actually going through the motions of smiling has been shown to improve your mood too, as it releases chemicals in the brain that are associated with pleasure and contentment.

Breathe in, to the count of three while imagining that the air comes in through holes in your feet. Feel the sensation of warmth and heaviness flowing through your body, starting at your feet and ending at your head.

Breathe out to the count of three. Visualise your breath passing through your body from your head and out through the holes in your feet. Feel the warmth and heaviness flow through your body. Let your muscles relax, let the jaw, tongue and shoulders go limp.

Now open your eyes and resume your normal activity.

Using BIOFEEDBACK to monitor your level of relaxation

Anxiety is composed of many bodily responses such as heart rate, blood pressure, muscle tenseness, skin temperature, sweating and brain electrical activity. 'Biofeedback' allows the user to see for himself the physiological level of their anxiety by using a variety of different measuring instruments. It is a useful tool for relaxation training, as it will indicate to the user whether or not a state of relaxation has been achieved.

THE BIODOT

A very simple and inexpensive biofeedback device is called the **biodot**.

Biodots are small, self-adhesive, temperature-sensitive discs that can be stuck to the skin. They indicate changes in skin temperature by changing colour. A brown colour will indicate that you are very tense and unsettled. A turquoise colour will show that you are beginning to relax, while a blue colour indicates calm. A violet colour is an indication that you are very relaxed.

How to use biodots

Carefully place the biodot on the back of your hand close to your thumb and forefinger, near your first knuckle. The biodot need only rest firmly on the skin, with the colour side facing you. Now look at the colour and see what state your body is in, relaxed or tense. The idea of using these biodots is to encourage you to relax more and more until the disc turns violet. The biodot gives you feedback about your biological reactions, which is why it is called a 'biofeedback' device. Keep focused on the colour and try to keep it violet for as long as you possibly can.

How do biodots monitor stress

When our bodies are relaxed they tend to generate more heat because the blood vessels at the surface of our skin dilate, releasing more heat. The biodot contains heat-sensitive chemicals which change colour at different temperatures. As our anxiety level increases, and our skin temperature decreases, the biodot begins to change to a turquoise and eventually a brown colour. As our anxiety level drops, it will begin changing to blue and eventually to violet as you reach maximum relaxation. So when our body is at normal temperature (94.6°F) the biodot colour will be violet and we will be very relaxed. At around 92.6°F it will be turquoise and we will be relaxing. At 90.6°F it will be yellow and we will be unsettled, and at 89.6°F will be amber-brown and we will be tense. At 87°F it will be black and we will be very tense.

The biodot is one of the most simplest biofeedback devices

in use today. Others include monitors for heart and breathing rates, brain waves, skin sweating and other physiological functions. So biofeedback can be used to control a number of different bodily functions including heart rate for people suffering from high blood pressure, and the brain waves of epileptics.

Factors affecting biodot colour

There are a number of different factors that can affect the temperature of the skin, which would therefore change the colour of the biodot. One of these is illness. When we have a cold or flu, or some type of infection, our skin temperature increases as our body's defences go into action. This will give a false reading on the biodot, as will taking a variety of drugs, including alcohol, panadol, aspirin and others. Other factors include the actual environmental temperature. Pregnant women tend to have different skin temperatures due to the various hormonal changes. If you are ill or are taking drugs, or are pregnant, then you should interpret the biodot reading with caution, or better still not use it at all until you return to your normal state.

THE NUTRITIONAL APPROACH

It was Hyppocrates, the 'Father of Physicians', who wisely said 2,500 years ago, **'Let food be thy medicine, and medicine be thy food.'**

It's unfortunate that very few modern-day physicians have taken heed of this. Hyppocrates was using natural ingredients to allow the body to heal itself, which is called the 'orthomolecular' approach to medicine (Gk. ortho - 'correct'; molecular - 'molecules' or 'substances'). So by providing those molecules or nutrients that the body lacks such as vitamins, minerals, fatty acids and amino acids along with an optimum diet, it is possible to restore the body's physical, psychological and spiritual balance and health. The opposite approach, widely practised by the majority of the medical profession, is the 'toximolecular' approach whereby various toxins or drugs which are foreign to the body are prescribed in the hope that they will help the illness being treated. These drugs may indeed help to alleviate the symptoms, but they always create other unwanted side-effects or iatrogenic (drug-induced) illnesses, an increasing problem in the twentieth century, particularly among the very young and the very old.

Personally, I do not believe that the use of tranquillisers to alleviate phobic anxiety is the answer. One problem with these drugs are the side effects, the most common being:

• *Drowsiness, accompanied by lack of concentration* - *a very common side-effect.*

• *Poor coordination* - *special care needs to be taken by those driving or working with machinery.*

• *Unsteadiness* - *very much like when you are drunk and cannot support yourself properly.*

• *Blurred vision* - *this is more common when coming off tranquillisers than when taking them regularly.*

• *Aggression* - *some people have shown uncharacteristic aggression and hostility, bewildering when it happens unexpectedly.*

Apart from the addiction and withdrawal effects of tranquillisers and hypnotics, there are certain benefits to using tranquillisers occasionally, after careful thought. If, for example, there is no other way of controlling your phobic anxiety in a given situation, such as when flying, then tranquillisers prescribed by a doctor can be quite helpful to calm and sedate you on the flight, but not continued over a long period of time.

However, if your anxiety is not so incapacitating, then I would strongly recommend taking natural remedies which will calm and alleviate the tension, without any side-effects, addictions or withdrawal symptoms. As these nutrients are natural substances found in food, by definition they do not need a prescription from a doctor. The secret is knowing which nutrients to take and in what combination, as their optimum effect occurs when they work synergistically, or as a team. Most of these natural remedies are freely available in chemists and health food shops in many European countries.

DIET AND ANXIETY

As Hyppocrates rightly said, food can be your medicine, if you know what type of food to eat, and when. The type of food you eat can either increase or decrease your anxiety. Some of the major stimulants, for example alcohol, coffee, chocolate, cola and cigarettes can exacerbate our anxiety levels. For example, alcohol can inhibit the mobilisation of reserve glucose from the liver and depress the demand for more sugar by a part of the brain called the hypothalamus, thus contributing to low blood sugar problems. Coffee contains theobromine, theophylline and caffeine, all of which act as stimulants. Caffeine stimulates the nervous system and the production of the catecholamines, particularly noradrenaline. Taking an excess amount of caffeine is like being in a state of high arousal, with the body reacting as if in an emergency situation, which burdens the body further over time. Caffeine can also increase the production of hydrochloric acid by the stomach, which on an empty stomach can lead to heartburn, indigestion and aggravate ulcers. Cocoa also contains theobromine, and cola drinks contain caffeine too. These also have a tendency to stimulate the pancreas which releases insulin, which again will reduce blood sugar levels.

Let us briefly look at the right type of foods to eat on board, and those that are best avoided.

In times of fear and anxiety it is always best to eat the following foods:

• **light, raw, fresh foods such as vegetables, fruit, nuts and seeds. Crunch on as much fruit, carrots, celery, almonds, walnuts, etc., that you like. These foods are truly good for you.**

Avoid the following:

• **acid-producing foods such as meat, fish and cheeses. It would also be wise to give a miss to all stimulants such as coffee, tea and alcohol. These tend to exacerbate the anxiety and stress reaction, as mentioned above. Tea, coffee and other caffeine-containing drinks such as cola and Lucozade can actually mimic some of the symptoms of anxiety, therefore setting up a vicious cycle.**

I suggest that you eat a light lunch or dinner on the aeroplane, and drink plenty of water. When you make your booking, request a vegetarian meal. This costs no extra, and will probably contain salad and fruit, excellent foods for our purposes. (Remember, it is too late to ask for a special meal when you arrive at the airport). Camomile tea is a natural relaxant, so take some tea-bags with you (the Cabin Crew will provide the hot water) and drink 3-4 cups of this throughout the flight.

It is best not to add sugar, as white sugar (sucrose) stimulates your pancreas to secrete insulin, which reduces your blood sugar levels rapidly. This may lead to low blood sugar which again mimics a lot of symptoms very similar to anxiety and tension. When the blood sugar level drops we may feel confused, forgetful, have difficulty concentrating, be impatient and irritable, develop headaches and emotional instability. These are all symptoms of the anxiety that we are trying to alleviate.

If we constantly eat sugar, the pancreas is continuously stimulated. The pancreas produces insulin which helps to take the sugar out of the blood and store it in the liver. If we eat any carbohydrate in refined form (white sugar, sweets, chocolate, white flour and its products, as well as stimulants such as caffeine and nicotine) digestion is rapid, and glucose enters the blood in a violent rush. In each case, the pancreas can over-react and produce too much insulin. This will lead to the blood sugar taking a very rapid nose-dive, and dropping too low for normal functioning.

This worsens your existing anxiety and fear. All the other stimulants mentioned above, as well as sugar and any sweet foods, can trigger a rapid drop in your blood sugar levels and so should be avoided, at least throughout the course of the flight. Remember that fruit juices contain sugar that is rapidly converted to glucose by the body. Try diluting juices with mineral water, or soda water. Try to eat small, frequent meals, preferably containing protein or complex carbohydrates such as fruit, wholewheat bread, pulses, nuts, vegetables and a little fish and meat.

THE NATURAL TRANQUILLISERS

Scientists have discovered that when we are anxious and stressed, our brain waves tend to speed up from their usual slow, relaxed alpha waves, to faster, more alert beta waves. There are many ways of slowing down these brain waves and therefore rebalancing the stress response.

Most people do this by taking tranquillisers such as Valium, Librium, Ativan, Xanax or the assortment of other trade names that exist. As we have already seen, all these will inevitably have some type of unwanted side effects, some of which include, dizziness, drowsiness, irritability, inability to concentrate and a general feeling of being unwell. What most people want to do when they are stressed and anxious is to relax, but at the same time be clear-headed, alert and focused. For many years physicians of old have pointed out that one of the best ways to resolve mind and body problems is to allow the natural rhythms of the body to deal with them. All we need to do is provide the nutrients that our body needs in order to manufacture its own tranquillising chemicals.

Over the last two or three decades, nutritionists and orthomolecular specialists have found natural substances to help alleviate anxiety. These occur naturally in food and include nutrients such as amino acids, vitamins, minerals, fatty acids and trace elements.

One amino acid that has been found to reduce the intensity of beta waves and encourage the growth of alpha waves is HISTIDINE. Histidine is the parent molecule of the highly active histamine, a substance that is required by the brain (as a neuro-inhibitor to reduce the intensity of beta waves). Stress generally reduces the levels of histamine available to the brain, resulting in the sort of irritability, uncertainty and mental confusion associated with a fear of flying. By taking histidine supplements (which are totally harmless) you can promote the alpha wave functions, calming and relaxing the mind when anxiety threatens to take a grip.

There are a number of other free amino acids that can also be used to alleviate anxiety. These include GLYCINE and TAURINE, which help to calm the involuntary physical agitation of anxiety.

For all amino acids to work, they need helpers (or 'co-factors', as they are called). For the above-mentioned amino acids these co-factors include some of the B vitamins, such as vitamins B1, B2 and B6, vitamin C, and zinc. A good multimineral/vitamin supplement would provide all these in good doses.

So, what can you take to help with your anxiety? I have already mentioned that the amino acids histidine, taurine and glycine play an important anxiety-reducing role. For these to work, some of the B-vitamins are required such as thiamine, inositol, riboflavin and pyridoxine, along with vitamin C. It would be possible to take each one of these nutrients separately but that would mean swallowing a lot of little pills. Instead, it is possible to take these in one capsule, named CALMA COMPLEX, a formula produced and manufactured by Advanced Nutrition Ltd*. This company also make another supplement that helps to alleviate anxiety, called BIO-REST, which contains calcium and magnesium, both known to provide a relaxing effect on the muscles, as well as other vital ingredients. Bio Science recommend that they should be taken together. I suggest that you take two Calma Complex and two Bio-Rest before the flight, and then one of each every hour up to five times. If this seems like a lot, don't worry. These are not drugs, they are food supplements that are totally harmless. They will simply help to alleviate your anxiety.

Dr Robert Erdmann, Director of Advanced Nutrition Ltd., reports that up to 10 Bio-Rest tablets can be taken at once and cites an example of their effectiveness:

'*A secretary who was so terrified of flying that she had never been up in an aeroplane was confronted with a pressing desire to make a trip which precluded any other means of transport. She took 4 Bio-Rest tablets with breakfast, 4 as she left for the airport, 4 when they arrived to check in, and 10 tablets about five minutes before boarding the aircraft. In the event, she enjoyed the flight. She repeated the dosage on the return journey, and felt completely relaxed. Later, she totally overcame her fear of flying and did not have to use any nutritional supplement, although she still found the tablets useful, in place of tranquillisers, for dealing with job-related anxieties*'.

*Calma Complex and Bio-Rest can be obtained by mail order from Advanced Nutrition Ltd, Broadway House, 14 Mount Pleasant Road, Tunbridge Wells, Kent, PN1 1QU, England, or from Bioscience, 2398 Alaska Avenue, Port Orchard, WA. 98366, USA.

I also recommend that you take a good multivitamin/ multimineral formula, such as Solgar's VM2000, Cantassium's Cantamega 2000, Lambert's Vitamin/Mineral Complex or Health Plus's VV Pack. Take these multimineral/vitamin tablets as prescribed on the package, along with the Calma Complex and Bio-Rest as suggested above. As a rough guide, a good multivitamin/mineral formula will contain at least 30-50mg B-complex vitamins, so look for this on the pack. If in doubt about any of these nutritional supplements, you can always ask your local nutritionist for further information.

Please note that the authors and the publishers cannot accept responsibility for anyone taking these remedies without the guidance of a qualified practitioner - these are only guidelines which the person reading will take ultimate responsibility for.

The effect of these nutrients is not going to be a sudden relaxation, as one would expect from a powerful tranquilliser. Instead, it will take a little while before you begin to feel the soothing effects - maybe half an hour or so, so you need to take these at least 30-60 minutes before the flight.

HERBAL FORMULAS
In addition to these nutritional supplements, that you could perhaps begin taking even a few days before the trip to ensure that your anxiety levels fall considerably before the flight, you could also take a good herbal formula, again readily available in tablet form from leading chemists and health food shops.

In Britain, there are a couple of products available that I know of. One is called **Natracalm** and contains a plant extract called Passiflora incarnata, commonly known as the Passion Flower. The other is **Valerina** which contains Valerian extract, Hops extract, Humulus lupules, Lemon balm extract and Melissa extract, all herbs scientifically known to have a sedative and tranquillising effect, without any side effects. Again, I suggest that you begin taking these a few days, or even a couple of weeks before your trip, in order to give your body some time to adjust to a new relaxed mode.

Generally, it is O.K. to take these herbs, but if in doubt, ask a qualified medical herbalist. Women who are pregnant or breast feeding should not take these herbs, or any others without prior expert advice. If you are on any type of drugs, DO NOT try to stop these by yourself without first consulting your prescribing doctor.

BACH FLOWER REMEDIES

I believe that everyone should read one of Dr. Bach's books - he was truly an amazing physician, pathologist, immunologist, bacteriologist, homeopath and researcher, but above all, he was an incredibly altruistic person. I use his remedies every day in my clinical practice with absolutely amazing results. I use them instead of tranquillisers and psychotropic (brain-changing) drugs.

One of the first personal experiences that I had with the Rescue Remedy, which I will talk about in a while, was with my children's pet chickens. They had apparently picked up some type of infection that was crippling them to death. The mother hen first had the problem, and this was passed on to her young chicks. One by one they began to die, so I decided quite instinctively to try the Rescue Remedy. As the young chick was lying on the ground with paralysed legs, looking very weak and helpless, I put 3-4 drops of Rescue Remedy in its mouth. Literally, within 5-10 seconds, it got up, shook itself, and shot off at an incredibly fast pace! I was absolutely amazed! I then tried this with the mother hen, and she also made immediate progress. Within the next couple of days the hen and her chicks were completely cured. This certainly was no placebo effect! I then had further experiences with plants that grew much healthier with Bach Flower Remedies, so I was truly convinced.

I will briefly mention a few of the remedies that I feel will be helpful in cases of fear, anxiety and panic below. Again, these are freely available in most chemists and health food stores.

ROCK ROSE - for extreme terror, panic, hysteria, fright and nightmares.

MIMULUS - for known fears, for example, flying, fear of heights, pain, darkness, death, etc. Also for timidity and shyness.

CHERRY PLUM - for fear of losing mental and physical control; inclination to uncontrollable rages and impulses, with fear of causing harm to oneself or others.

ASPEN - for vague fears and anxieties of unknown origin, a sense of foreboding, apprehension, or impending disaster.

I suggest that you buy all 4 of these remedies, buy a 30ml amber medicine bottle with dropper, fill this with mineral water, and then place 2 drops of each remedy into the bottle. Shake it up, and take 4 drops, 4 times daily. Begin this a few weeks before your trip, and I am certain that all will go well.

There is one final remedy which is an absolute must!

RESCUE REMEDY

Rescue Remedy was named by Dr. Bach for its calming and stabilising effect on the emotions during a crisis. This is why it is ideally suited for flying fears, and for any imbalance in the psychological or emotional state of a person, as often occurs during an anxiety or panic attack.

Rescue Remedy is made up of the following five Bach Flower remedies:

IMPATIENS - for the impatience, irritability, and agitation often accompanying stress. This may sometimes result in muscle tension and pain.

CLEMATIS - for unconsciousness, spaciousness, faintness, and out-of-the-body sensations, which often accompany trauma.

ROCK ROSE for terror, panic, hysteria, and great fear.

CHERRY PLUM for fear of losing mental or physical control.

STAR OF BETHLEHEM for trauma, both mental and physical.

Rescue Remedy can be used in combination with the other remedies already mentioned. Rescue Remedy has been shown to be non-toxic, non-habit-forming, and free from side effects. However, it should be noted that Rescue Remedy is not meant to be a panacea or a substitute for emergency medical treatment.

You may buy the Rescue Remedy in a liquid concentrate form. Place four drops of this concentrate into a quarter glass of liquid. Sip every 3-5 minutes or more often as necessary. Hold in mouth a moment before swallowing.

If water or other beverages are not available, then Rescue Remedy may be taken directly from the concentrate bottle by placing 4 drops under the tongue. Drops may also be added to a spoonful of water if desired.

For those unable to drink, the remedy may be rubbed directly from the concentrate bottle on the lips, behind the ears, or on the wrists. The Rescue Remedy is also available in cream form, which again can be rubbed on the skin, where it will be directly absorbed.

There is absolutely no reason why you should not be able to lie back and enjoy a quiet, peaceful trip, free from anxiety, fear and tension. These symptoms are not all in the mind; they are true physiological reactions of the body that can now be controlled using a nutritional and natural approach. There is no real need to dose up with tranquillisers, which have all the unpleasant side-effects that are not really conducive to a relaxed and enjoyable flight. Should you want to find out more about your health from a natural and nutritional perspective, and other ways that you may help to optimise your health using natural means, then I suggest that you visit a qualified nutritionist/ herbalist/naturopath/natural therapist at the next available opportunity. These therapists will be able to assess your existing health and develop a short and long term health programme that will help to optimise your health. Maybe one of the reasons that you have a variety of fears, including a fear of flying, is because you have a sugar imbalance problem, or are deficient in some of the B-vitamins that keep the nervous system in a healthy balance, or you may be low on magnesium, calcium, or potassium, all of which can create a variety of mental symptoms. This can be cured using a nutritional approach, under the guidance of a qualified nutritional/natural therapist.

The natural therapies that I have mentioned are by no means exhaustive. There are many other types of therapies that could be sought such as homeopathy, aromatherapy, meditation, etc., but I have tried to be as practical as possible in giving suggestions that can be implemented while actually on the flight. Indeed, a qualified Clinical Psychologist or Behavioural Therapist would be able to use other psychological and cognitive therapeutic techniques such as systematic desensitisation to help a person's flying fears - but we are talking about a few months of therapy. And even then, if the person has other nutritional imbalances such as blood sugar problems and does not eat correctly, this may not be totally effective. So the suggestions I have made are practical and easily implementable whilst on board a plane, but do not look into other therapies if your phobia is truly incapacitating.

To summarise the potential things that one can do or take, the therapies have been outlined in brief in Appendix 3.

Finally, I sincerely hope that this little section on how to decrease your anxiety has worked for you, and that you may even have enjoyed your flight. If, however, you found that there was simply nothing that you could do to help yourself as your anxiety level was so high, perhaps it would be a good idea when you are on the ground to visit a natural therapist of the kind mentioned above. They should be able to help you cure both your phobia and your anxiety once and for all.

For those that have benefited from the book, I would love to hear from you, or even see you if you happen to be flying to Cyprus, at the following address:

Dr. George J. Georgiou, BSc, MSc, Ph. D, C. Biol, C. Psychol, FAACS, AFBPsS, MIBiol, R.Ir., M.G.N.I.
NATURAL THERAPY CENTRE,
P.O. Box 2008,
6530 Larnaca,
CYPRUS.
Tel: + + 357 4 659520
Fax: + + 357 4 624434
e-mail: drgeorge@zenon.logos.cy.net

Good luck, happy flying, and God bless!

Appendix 1

SUMMARY OF THINGS TO DO

- POSITIVE IMAGERY
 - think positive, feel positive

- BREATH CORRECTLY
- fundamental to relaxation

- QUIETING REFLEX
- easy relaxation technique

- USE THE BIODOTS
- biofeedback device

- NUTRITIONAL SUPPLEMENTS
- the natural way to relax

- HERBS
- can be an alternative to tranquilisers

- BACH FLOWER REMEDIES
- natural way of controlling your emotions

- RESCUE REMEDY
- an absolute must for all Aerophobics!

- DIET - EAT CORRECTLY
- eat the correct foods in flight to help keep the body balanced

Appendix 2

Ten Golden Rules for Taking the Fear out of Flying

These were formulated by the late Dr Maurice Yaffé, the Psychological Director of the Air Travel Anxiety Seminar, a programme aimed at helping people suffering from apprehension about flying. Readers might like to buy Dr Yaffé's excellent book, available in paperback from most British airport bookstalls. It is called 'Taking the Fear out of Flying'.

DR MAURICE YAFFE'S 10 GOLDEN RULES FOR TAKING THE FEAR OUT OF FLYING

Remember:

1. When flying is viewed as a threat, panicky feelings are often the result. Don't worry: these are normal - albeit exaggerated - reactions. Avoidance or escape only keep the problem going; they do not help resolve it.

2. Nothing worse can happen to you. All that follows anxiety is relaxation.

3. Focus on the here-and-now, and what is actually happening. The future will take care of itself.

4. Monitor your breathing and make sure your pattern is slow and relatively deep - as opposed to fast and shallow. Don't hold your breath.

5. Adopt the view that everything is normal unless you are told absolutely and incontrovertibly otherwise by those who know, i.e. the professional flight crew.

6. Give yourself permission to be here. Adopt the view that you have nothing better to do than go through with the experience. Remember the reasons which made you decide to confront the situation in the first place.

7. Feelings follow behaviour rather than the reverse: you have to attend to what happens on a flight to feel better about it. So, for example, look out of the cabin window in order to become comfortable about it. Don't wait to feel in the mood to do so.

8. Take positive action. Start to relax as soon as you feel any signs of tension or anxiety, or if for any reason the level increases.

9. Don't jump to conclusions. What is the hard evidence on which you are basing your negative views? Are there alternative explanations for what you are thinking?

10. At the end of the trip, note down how it really was - NOT what you think it should have been like. Highlight what helped, and what you need to attend to next time. On your next flight, take a brief list of 'personal statements'. Learning to feel comfortable about flying is a skill like any other, and so practice is necessary to get it completely right. Taking another flight within a few weeks is likely to speed up the process.

Dr Yaffé's book 'Taking the Fear out of Flying' is available at bookshops and airports.

Appendix 3

STILL UNEASY ABOUT FLYING?

COURSES (IN THE UNITED KINGDOM)

1. If you would like to learn more, or still feel apprehensive about flying, Aviatours Ltd, together with British Airways, run special courses that are designed to reassure you and make your next flight more relaxing and enjoyable. These one-day courses include a short flight and are run by two highly experienced British Airways pilots and a trained psychologist. To find out more, please contact: Aviatours Ltd., 'Pinewoods', Eglinton Road, Tilford, Surrey GU10 2DH. Tel: 01252-793250.

2. Flight Simulator. Emily Jacob runs individual therapy courses in London, sometimes involving the use of a flight simulator. Contact: Emily Jacob, tel: 0181-878-58353.

3. Britannia Airways run occasional courses at East Midlands airport, similar to the Aviatours course mentioned above. Contact: Brenda McMichael, Britannia Airways, Luton Airport, Beds, LU2 9ND.

BOOKS, TAPES

1. Plane Scared is a useful, 11 page booklet produced to accompany Channel 4 TV's documentary of the same name. To order a copy, send £1 (cheques/P.O.'s made payable to Channel 4 Television) to Plane Scared, P.O. Box 4000, London W3 6XJ.

2. Fly Without Fear is a tape produced by Lifeskills Ltd, who also offer individual counselling. The tapes cost £8.50 + £1.00 post and packing. Contact: Lifeskills Ltd., Bowman House, 6 Billetsfield, Taunton TA1 3NN.

3. Taking the Fear out of Flying. Dr Maurice Yaffé's book, published by David and Charles. Available from booksellers, or by mail order for £8.50, including post & packing, from

Aviatours (see address above).

4. A video, Are you Afraid to Fly?, costing £14.50, and a booklet of the same title, costing £5, (both including post and packing), are available from Aviatours (see address above).

MEDICAMENT
The writer is not qualified to comment on the advisability or suitability of tranquillisers, etc, but a homeopathic practitioner advised him that the homeopathic remedy 'Aconite' is effective. One 200c tablet should be taken on the morning of a flight, and another just before the trip starts.

BIBLIOGRAPHY

If you are interested in reading more about alternative approaches to health, Dr Georgiou recommends the following books that you could read to expand your interests:

• Beck, A.T. and Emery, G et al. *Anxiety Disorders and Phobias: A Cognitive Perspective.* New York: Basic Books, Inc., Publishers, (1985).

• Erdmann, R. & Jones, M. *The Amino Revolution: The most exciting development in nutrition since the vitamin tablet.* UK: Century Hutchinson Ltd., 1989.

• Hanson, P. *The Joy of Stress.* UK: Pan Books, 1988.

• Holford, P. *Optimum Nutrition Workbook: All the Facts You Need to Know for a Healthy Life.* UK: ION Press, 1992.

• Looker, T. & Gregson, O. *Stresswise: A Practical Guide for Dealing with Stress.* UK: Hodder and Stoughton Educational, 1989.

• Murray, M. & Pizzorno, J. *Encyclopaedia of Natural Medicine.* UK: Macdonald Optima, 1992.

• Ody, P. *The Herb Society's Complete Medicinal Herbal.* UK: Dorling Kindersley, 1993.

• Ramsell, J. *Questions and Answers: The Bach Flower Remedies.* UK: The C. W. Daniel Company Limited, 1991.

• Trattler, R. *Better Health Through Natural Healing.* UK: Thorsons, 1985.

• Vlamis, G. *Rescue Remedy: The Healing Power of Bach Flower Rescue Remedy.* UK: Thorsons, 1994.

BIOGRAPHIES

Adrian Akers-Douglas is a former RAF and Cyprus Airways pilot, who now flies Airbus A320's for Eurocypria Airlines. He lives in Cyprus.

Dr. Georgiou has a BSc (combined honours) degree in Biology/Psychology (U.K.), and a Ph.D. in Clinical Sexology from the U.S.A. He is also a Licensed Nutritionist (DipION), a Registered Iridologist (R.Ir) and is presently studying Naturopathy and Herbal Medicine.

He has been an active clinician for 15 years, is Director of the Natural Therapy Centre in Larnaca/Nicosia, Cyrpus, which specialises in Natural Health, and includes Medicine, Nutrition, Chelation, Naturopathy, Herbal Medicine, Iridology, Psychotherapy, and Sex Therapy - a truly holistic approach.

He has been the Principle Investigator for the World Health Organisation in studies on AIDS and Drug Use, as well as other psychosocial studies. He is Academic Coordinator and lecturer of the Masters in Psychology Course (Clinical Emphasis) at a private college in Cyprus, and has been a prolific writer of health articles for the general public, as well as having his own radio programme on the island for 2 years entitled *Human Sexuality*. He has been an Aviation Consultant/Human Factors and Crew Resource Management Programme Developer and Facilitator Trainer for a number of years to Cyprus Airways and EuroCypria, given that he is also a keen Private Pilot himself (hence the interest in this book).

He is an Associate Fellow of the British Psychology Society (AFBPsS), a registered Chartered Clinical Psychologist (C. Clin. Psychol.), a Chartered Biologist (C. Biol.) and Member of the Institute of Biology (MIBiol.), a Diplomate of the American Board of Sexology (ABS), and a Certified Sex Therapist, a Fellow of the American Academy of Clinical Sexologists (FAACS), a Member of the Nutrition Consultants Association and the Council for Nutrition Education and Therapy (CNEAT) and a Member of the Guild of Naturopathic Iridologists (M.G.N.I.). He is also an elected liaison person for representing Cypriot

Clinical Psychologists in Europe.

Dr. Georgiou is married to a Psychologist with two children, and enjoys art, nature, ecological and natural approaches to health, antiques, tropical fish, flying, reading and the family.

Matt Wilde lives in Cyprus and does his own thing.

Index

OTHER BOOKS FROM SUMMERSDALE

TRAVEL

Zen Explorations in Remotest New Guinea
Adventures in the Jungles and Mountains of Irian Jaya, Neville Shulman
138 x 222mm 160pp ISBN 1 84024 005 9
£12.99 Hardback

Two Feet, Four Paws (New Edition)
The Girl Who Walked Her Dog 4500 Miles, Spud Talbot-Ponsonby
216 x 135mm 256pp ISBN 1 84024 002 4
£6.99 Paperback

The Sea On Our Left
A couple's ten month walk around Britain's coastline, Shally Hunt
216 x 135mm 288pp ISBN 1 873475 96 9
£7.99 Paperback

Making Movies
Tales and travels across the American Filmscape, Phillip Turner
216 x 135mm 256pp ISBN 1 84024 004 0
£7.99 Paperback

Don't Lean Out Of The Window! (New Edition)
The Inter-Rail Experience, Stewart Ferris and Paul Bassett
216 x 135mm 192pp ISBN 1 84024 003 2
£5.99 Paperback

And Mother Came Too
Joy Viney
216 x 135mm 160pp ISBN 1 873475 35 7
£5.99 Paperback

SCIENCE FICTION

The MiXtake Files
A nit-picker's guide to The X-Files, Michael French
230 x 190mm 160pp ISBN 1 84024 008 3
£9.99 Paperback

The Book of Star Wars Trivia
Robert Bircher and Rachel Coulthurst
230 x 190mm 160pp ISBN 1 84024 024 5
£9.99 Paperback

CREATIVE WRITING

Bestsellers
The Art of Writing Blockbusters - by the Bestselling Authors in the World
240 x 160mm 288pp ISBN 1 84024 009 1
£15.99 Hardback

Writing From Experience
A step-by-step approach to freelance writing, Amanda Wilkins
216 x 135mm 96pp ISBN 1 873475 89 6
£4.99 Paperback

Overcoming Rejection
A Sales Course For The As Yet Unpublished, Edward Baker
216 x 135mm 160pp ISBN 1 84024 010 5
£7.99 Paperback

Write Your Life
A Guide to Autobiography, Ken Moon
210 x 135mm 163pp ISBN 0 947351 96 5
£8.99 Paperback

Writing Quality Fiction
Ken and Elaine Moon
210 x 135mm 163pp ISBN 1 875857 21 4
£8.99 Paperback

BIOGRAPHY

Gracie Fields
A Biography, Joan Moules
135 x 216mm 256pp ISBN 1 84024 001 6
£7.99 Paperback

Yes, Mr Bronson
Memoirs of a Bum Actor, Michael Sheard
216 x 135mm 256pp ISBN 1 84024 007 5
£6.99 Paperback

During The War
And other encounters, Buster Merryfield
216 x 135 mm 256pp ISBN 1 873475 54 3
£4.99 Paperback

HEALTH

Shaping Up During and After Pregnancy
Dr Stavia Blunt
245 x 190mm 160pp ISBN 1 84024 013 X
£9.99 Paperback

TRUE CRIME

The Many Faces of Jack the Ripper
M.J. Trow
215 x 270mm 192pp ISBN 1 84024 016 4
£15.99 Hardback

COOKERY

The Bachelor's Cookbook
Easy Cooking For Men, Alastair Williams
216 x 135mm 160pp ISBN 1 84024 012 1
£5.99 Paperback

The Student Grub Guide
Alastair Williams
216 x 135 mm 160pp ISBN 1 873475 24 1
£4.99 Paperback

The Vegetarian Student Grub Guide
Alastair Williams
216 x 135 mm 160pp ISBN 1 873475 69 1
£4.99 Paperback

Cooking in the Nude (Volume 3)
Playful Gourmets, Stephen and Debbie Cornwell
225 x 154mm 96pp ISBN 0 943231 97 3
£6.99 Paperback

SELF DEFENCE

Dead Or Alive - The Choice Is Yours
The Definitive Self Protection Handbook, Geoff Thompson
245 x 190mm 256pp ISBN 1 873475 36 5
£12.99 Paperback

The Modern Bodyguard   (New Edition)
The Manual of Close Protection Training, Peter Consterdine
240 x 170 mm 316pp ISBN 1 873475 09 8
£24.99 Paperback

BUSINESS

How To Start In Business
The Guide to Succeeding in Business, Guy A. Allen
216 x 135mm 160pp ISBN 1 873475 47 0
£6.99 Paperback

How To Develop Your Business
The Guide to Successful Business Expansion, Guy A. Allen
216 x 135mm 160pp ISBN 1 873475 57 8
£6.99 Paperback

The Art of Telemarketing
How to Sell by Telephone, Helen Kelman
216 x 135mm 96pp ISBN 1 84024 023 7
£6.99 Paperback 31st October 1997

EFL/LANGUAGES

The EFL Directory 1998
The Complete Guide to Learning English in Britain, Europa Pages
216 x 135mm 144pp ISBN 1 84024 014 8
£6.99 Paperback

The French Directory 1998
The Complete Guide to Learning French in France, Europa Pages
216 x 135mm 116pp ISBN 1 84024 015 6
£6.99 Paperback

RELATIONSHIPS

The Good Dating Guide
The Do's and Don'ts of Dating, Hillie Marshall
216 x 135mm 160pp ISBN 1 84024 017 2
£7.99 Paperback

Agonise With Hillie
Solutions from Hillie Marshall
216 x 135mm 160pp ISBN 1 873475 80 2
£6.99 Paperback

Hillie Marshall's Guide to Successful Relationships
216 x 135 mm 160pp ISBN 1 873475 33 0
£6.99 Paperback

HUMOUR

Kama Sutra For One
The Single Man's Guide to Self-Satisfaction, Dr O'Nan & Palm
108 x 200mm 128pp ISBN 1 84024 025 3
£3.99 Paperback

How To Chat-up Men (New Edition)
Amy Mandeville
216 x 135mm 160pp ISBN 1 84024 022 9
£4.99 Paperback

How To Chat-up Women
Stewart Ferris
216 x 135mm 160pp ISBN 1 873475 83 7
£4.99 Paperback

Chat-up Lines and Put downs
Stewart Ferris
108 x 135mm 128pp ISBN 1 84024 020 2
£3.99 Paperback

Girl Power
The Smart Woman's Handbook, Kitty Malone
108 x 135mm 128pp ISBN 1 84024 021 0
£3.99 Paperback

101 Uses for a Losing Lottery Ticket
£3.99 Paperback

101 Ways to Spend Your Lottery Millions
£3.99 Paperback

Paws For Thought:
Another Purrfect Day, Pat Ashforth and Steve Plummer
110 x 176mm 64pp ISBN 1 84024 018 0
£3.99 Paperback

Paws For Thought:
It's A Dog's Life, Pat Ashforth and Steve Plummer
110 x 176mm 64pp ISBN 1 84024 019 9
£3.99 Paperback

A full catalogue of available titles can be obtained free of charge by writing to the publishers at:
Summersdale Publishers
46 West Street
Chichester
West Sussex
PO19 1RP
UK

All Summersdale titles can be obtained through your local bookshop. In case of difficulty, books can be ordered direct from Summersdale at the above address. Please state clearly which titles/quantities you require and enclose a cheque to cover the price of the book(s) plus £1 towards postage and packing per book for UK addresses (£3 per book overseas). Please make cheques/postal orders payable to: SUMMERSDALE PUBLISHERS.